THE SHAAR PRESS

THE JUDAICA IMPRINT
FOR THOUGHTFUL PEOPLE

Balanced

A SHAAR
PRESS
PUBLICATION

Parenting

her and a son – a rabbi and a psychologist –
ine love and limits in raising children

Rabbi Raphael Pelcovitz
Dr. David Pelcovitz

Published by **SHAAR PRESS**
Distributed by MESORAH PUBLICATIONS, LTD.
4401 Second Avenue / Brooklyn, N.Y 11232 / (718) 921-9000 / www.artscroll.com

Distributed in Israel by SIFRIATI / A. GITLER
6 Hayarkon Street / Bnei Brak 51127

Distributed in Europe by LEHMANNS
Unit E, Viking Business Park, Rolling Mill Road / Jarrow, Tyne and Wear, NE32 3DP/ England

Distributed in Australia and New Zealand by GOLDS WORLD OF JUDAICA
3-13 William Street / Balaclava, Melbourne 3183 / Victoria Australia

Distributed in South Africa by KOLLEL BOOKSHOP
Shop 8A Norwood Hypermarket / Norwood 2196, Johannesburg, South Africa

ISBN: 1-4226-0000-9 Hard Cover
ISBN: 1-4226-0001-7 Paperback

Printed in the United States of America by Noble Book Press
Custom bound by Sefercraft, Inc. / 4401 Second Avenue / Brooklyn N.Y. 11232

This volume is dedicated
to the memory of our beloved parents

Gwendolyn and Joseph Straus ז״ל

יוסף שמואל בן בנימין ז״ל

גיננדל בת משה יעקב ע״ה

Both were wonderful parents —
not only in what they said
but in the examples they set.
They showed us that people should live
not only for themselves.
Philanthropy, Israel, yeshivot —
these were the causes that permeated our family.

This book is a fitting memorial to them
because it will help craft and refine
the bonds between parents and children.

Zahava and Moshael Straus

Publishers' Preface

G randparents and senior educators lament that it is harder to raise children today than it has ever been. Social critics scoff that it has always been so: that the "good old days" always seem better in nostalgia than they were in reality. They insist that it was never easy to raise children, but the species has survived.

Nevertheless, it cannot be denied that the authority of parents, educators, and tradition has rarely, if ever, been so seriously (and successfully) challenged as in recent years. In a society where "truth" is relative, the teaching of "values" is expelled from school systems, and standards of acceptable behavior are constantly defined downward, the parent-child relationship must be given a new focus by people who bridge generations and who are fully conversant with past and present.

This book is unique in that it is a collaboration by two people who have earned universal respect in their fields, and who represent a combination of generations and areas of wisdom. There is a special symbolism in the fact that the authors are father and son, for they are proof that generations can and should enrich one another by sharing their knowledge and experience.

RABBI RAPHAEL PELCOVITZ, one of the country's most respected rabbis, has been renowned for more than half a century of distinguished service in Far Rockaway's famous "White Shul." During those years he has helped people with every conceivable problem by utilizing his Torah knowledge and perspective to illuminate the dark corners of their lives.

DAVID PELCOVITZ, PH.D. is a highly regarded psychologist who, in addition to conducting his private practice, has written and lectured extensively on the many aspects of parenting and on the problems asssociated with childhood and adolescence. Recently Dr. Pelcovitz was appointed to the Gwendolyn and Joseph Straus Chair in Jewish Education at both Yeshiva University's Azriel Graduate School of Jewish Education and Administration and Stern College for Woman.

This collaboration of two such highly regarded experts is a very successful blend of skill, judgment, and practical wisdom — an achievement that will be of invaluable assistance to countless families and educators.

It is fitting that this volume is dedicated by ZAHAVA AND MOSHAEL STRAUS, who endowed the academic chair now held by Dr. Pelcovitz. Mr. and Mrs. Straus are justly admired for their imaginative and generous role in enhancing Jewish life and Torah education. We are proud to welcome them to the "family" of those who make it possible to publish works of importance and enduring value such as *Balanced Parenting*.

We are grateful to our very dear friend RABBI RAPHAEL BUTLER, of the Afikim Foundation, who unselfishly brings imagination, vitality, and vision to his efforts to foster Torah values in Jewish life. This book was his concept and he helped immeasurably to bring it to reality.

Balanced Parenting is filled with practical advice leavened with the perspective of Judaism eternal. We have no doubt that it will be a valuable contribution to Jewish life.

Acknowledgments

The Hebrew word *horim* — parents — implies "teachers." We learned about parenting from the best possible teachers — our own parents. This book is therefore dedicated to the memory of Rabbi Ephraim and Necha Pelcovitz and Frumi Pelcovitz, *zichronam livracha*, who exemplified the lessons contained in this book.

We would like to express sincere appreciation to Rabbi Meir Zlotowitz, who inspired this book and encouraged us to see it through to a successful conclusion. We also want to express our gratitude to Rabbi Nosson Scherman, who skillfully edited *"The Parenting Path,"* the foundation and forerunner of this work. In addition, we wish to thank Rabbis Avraham Biderman and Mendy Herzberg for their invaluable assistance in the production phase of this project.

We gratefully recognize the vital contribution and tireless encouragement of Rabbi Raphael Butler, the moving force behind this venture. We are delighted to credit him for his creativity and the gentle prodding that gave the authors the all-too-rare luxury of spending many enjoyable hours working together while writing this book.

We are eternally grateful to our daughter and sister, Mrs. Ethel Gottlieb, for her careful and creative editing, which was done with great love and sincerity. Her wisdom and success in raising her own children and grandchildren, coupled with her erudition, her helpful suggestions and beneficial ideas are reflected throughout this volume.

Needless to say, the constant love, support, guidance, and parenting examples of our wives — Shirley and Lani, are the main inspiration for this book and for all that is worthwhile in our lives.

TABLE OF CONTENTS

Introduction

This book, which is an expansion of a previously published booklet, *The Parenting Path,* is a collection of thoughts and recommendations on parenting that emerged from a series of discussions between a father and son over the last several years. The father, Rabbi Ralph Pelcovitz, enriched by over 60 years as a rabbi, teacher and author, focused on the Torah perspective. The son, a clinical child-psychologist with over 25 years of experience as a clinician, researcher and teacher in a teaching hospital, integrated his father's insights with his understanding of current thinking on parenting in the child psychology literature.

The Talmud states:

Ulla Rabbah lectured at the entrance to the Nasi's house. What is meant by, "All the kings of the earth shall acknowledge You, for they have heard the words of Your mouth (Psalms 139:4)"? ... When the Holy One, Blessed is He, proclaimed, "I am Hashem your God, and you shall not have [other gods before Me]," the nations of the world said: He teaches merely for His own honor. As soon as He declared: "Honor your father and your mother," they recanted and acknowledged the first (two) statements (Kiddushin 31a).

This passage in the Talmud teaches us about the pivotal role that parenting plays in the world. The *Dibros* (Ten Commandments) have a logical dichotomy: The first five deal with man's relationship with God, and the last five with man's relationship to man.

What is it that joins the two? It is the fifth commandment, *Honor your father and your mother* (*Exodus* 20:12), that provides the bridge that makes parenting such an essential part of life. As the Talmud tells us, there are three partners involved in raising a child — the father, the mother and God. It is through parenting that we have the ultimate synthesis of the connection between God and man and between man and man.

At one point in the *davening* for the High Holy Days, when the *chazan* says the word "*ayeh*" (*where*) in *Kedushah,* we are given the opportunity to silently choose one of three special blessings: One can ask God for either Divine inspiration, sustenance, or good, proper and worthy children. When audiences at parenting lectures are asked what their silent choice is, virtually the unanimous assertion that they instinctively ask for is good, proper and worthy chidlren. What is uppermost in all of our hearts is the dream that our children turn out to be adults who are good, proper and worthy; adults who have internalized Torah values in their relationship between themselves and God and between themselves and others. Unfortunately, in today's complex world it is increasingly difficult to know how to raise our children in a manner that maximizes the chances that they will grow up to become truly "good, proper and worthy."

There is a surprising degree of agreement among psychologists about what constitute the central ingredients in successfully raising children. There are a number of studies that follow children from childhood through young adulthood with the aim of answering a basic question: "What differentiates parents who produce a *mentch*, an empathic, decent individual with the right kind of values, from parents who don't?" Surprisingly, for a field in which there is often dissension and conflicting opinions, the findings of these studies are consistent regarding the core characteristics that comprise successful child-rearing. Essentially, the distilled wisdom of these studies boil down to what our Rabbis taught us: The key to raising successful children is to find the balance between "the left hand pushing away while the right hand draws closer" (*Sanhedrin* 107b). This balance between love and limits is far more difficult to achieve in today's complicated world then ever before. A balancing act, which in previous generations might have been achieved intuitively and without much guidance, is far more difficult to accomplish in a society where parents are faced with greater challenges than their predecessors. They are often stressed and harried because of the financial demands that typically accompany raising large families, coupled with the increasing exposure of our children — through an increasingly pervasive media, such as the Internet — to a host of destructive influences. The purpose of this book is to present parents with some thoughts from a rabbi and a psychologist, who are also father and son, aimed at providing a toolbox of techniques and perspectives that might prove helpful in learning how to achieve the delicate balance between *the left hand that pushes away and the right hand that draws closer.*

Should a person tell you there is wisdom among the nations, believe it ... But if he tells you that there is Torah among the nations, do not believe it (Midrash Rabbah, Lamentations II:13).

From this *midrash* we see that from the Torah's point of view we do not dismiss or denigrate the wisdom of the world. As the *midrash* suggests, the benchmark is the teachings of the Torah. Our way of life is ultimately determined by the world-view of the Torah, not by the wisdom of the world. The way a person should conduct himself in real life is dictated by the truth of Torah, which is eternal and unchanging, rather than by the wisdom of the world which, in the case of psychology, is particularly transitory. In the realm of psychology in general, and parenting in particular, what was considered absolutely true and correct 50 years ago has given way to a whole new set of "truths" in current thinking. A prime example is Dr. Benjamin Spock, the pediatrician whose "bible" on childcare, *Baby and Childcare,* was perhaps the most influential guide to parenting in the secular world in the last half century. In earlier versions of his book, which was translated into 39 languages and ultimately sold more than 50 million copies, he counseled mothers never to pick up their infants when they cried. His belief, based on the prevailing wisdom of the time, was that to do so would irrevocably spoil the infant, who, he feared, would then grow up to be an overly indulged child and adolescent. Thankfully, mothers of that era followed their instincts, and secretly cuddled and held their crying babies, albeit while harboring guilt at ignoring the expert advice. Today, psychologists recognize that it would have been disastrous had Spock's advice been followed. Babies need physical contact with their parents and research has shown that without such holding and nurturing they are at increased risk for later difficulties, such as aggression and problems with intimacy. Later editions of Spock's book corrected this error. This is but one of numerous examples of the ephemeral wisdom of psychology.

In contrast, in the realm of morality and ethics we believe there are fundamental truths, which are based on human nature and that are implanted in us by the Creator. These are the same today as they were when Adam and Chavah were created. Man's temperament, inclinations, weaknesses and strengths are no different today than they were thousands of years ago. However, how man deals with these conflicting and challenging inclinations, as well as his interrelationship with the rest of the world, changes with the circumstances and forces of the world around us. Judaism has always taught us that even though the *emes* (truth) of Torah is constant, the way we respond to the human experience cannot be static, since the challenges we face and the nature of society are constantly in a state of flux.

Our Sages were great students of human psychology, even though they used different terminology than the jargon of modern-day psychologists. The teachers of ethical values had an uncanny ability to understand the human psyche and to appreciate the subtleties of human behavior. They had great insight into human motivation as reflected in their interpretation of the responses from a Torah perspective of our ancestors and of our great teachers. It should come as no surprise that psychologists today are only beginning to arrive at many of the conclusions and techniques described by the ethical teachers hundreds of years ago. In this book we have tried to meld the two: the teachings of Torah and its religious outlook with the insights of psychology. There is a fortuitous crossroad between Torah and the secular wisdom of psychology. The two together can offer profound insights into the nature and process of parenting.

This book is divided into three sections.

The first section examines some of the tools and ingredients involved in the application of love in a manner that captures the essence of *the right hand drawing closer*. The four chapters in this section examine the different facets that are involved in making a child feel loved and nurtured. In an era in which time is often at a premium, strategies for prioritizing time with your child are accompanied by practical suggestions on how to "steal" it from other less crucial endeavors. In an increasingly high-pressure community and educational environment it is particularly difficult to find ways to nurture a child's uniqueness. In the spirit of *Educate the youth according to his way (Proverbs 22:6)*, guidance is provided to show parents how to approach children with different temperaments, using different styles of parenting for each unique situation. Similarly, chapters discussing strategies on how to motivate children and instill values in a manner that promotes a maximum level of internalization help sensitize parents to the importance and complexity of these components of bringing our children close to us.

The second section of the book focuses on various aspects of calmly instituting appropriate limit-setting in a manner that properly captures the meaning of "the left hand pushing away." Perhaps the most frequently cited comment heard from educators and child mental-health professionals in recent years is that parents of this generation are "drawing closer" specialists. They are often far more comfortable with raising their children in a loving atmosphere than they are with the perhaps more difficult job of facing their children's discomfort and anger due to imposition of parental limits. The chapter on limit setting summarizes the dangers of not giving children the comfort and structure of appropriate limits, while the chapter on anger management in dealing with children provides some recommendations on how to deliver limits in a calm and effective manner. In the 1950's the Satmar Rebbe commented that his *chassidim* saw more of the "real world" in a subway ride from Williamsburg to Manhattan than their grandparents saw in a lifetime in the *shtetl*. One can only imagine how much more serious the challenge of raising children is in an environment dominated by far more extensive exposure to dangerous and enticing influences. With the advent of the Internet and other media, parents are often at a loss how to inoculate their children against pervasive and insidious external influences. The chapter on external influences provides some practical recommendations about taking an active and effective stand in this aspect of "the left hand pushing away." Finally, this section ends with a discussion on how parents can help their children cultivate the proper kinds of friendships while developing strategies for dealing with both overt and subtle forms of peer pressure.

The third section of the book provides some guidance on a number of additional topics that parents often face in our increasingly complex world. In the shadow of 9/11 and continuing terror in Israel, parents must often confront the challenge of providing their children with the appropriate balance of information, support and protection in efforts to help children cope with the impact of loss or disaster. The complex challenges of parenting children faced with chronic illness or loss of a family member are also addressed. A number of recommendations are made in this area, drawing from the enormous wisdom the Torah provides on dealing with tragedy. During the last decade, Jewish parents have also become increasingly aware of the issues of the at-risk adolescent who rebels against parental and religious guidance. Some of the current thinking about the sources of these problems is summarized, as well as some recommendations for parents and the community regarding how to recognize and intervene when faced with this problem. Finally, chapters on instilling one's child with respect for others as well as appropriate respect for themselves through a healthy self-concept provide a conclusion and an integration of the concepts and skills reviewed in this book.

There is a fascinating *gematria* (numerical equivalence based on the Hebrew alphabet) that captures the essence of the psychological experience of parenting. The numerical equivalent of the Hebrew words *ahavah* (אהבה, *love*) and *daagah* (דאגה, *worry*) are identical (13). Parenting a child is an experience that, at its core, involves a mixture of love intertwined with worry. It is our hope that this book helps reduce this anxiety by providing some measure of insight, guidance and encouragement.

PART ONE

THE RIGHT HAND DRAWING CLOSER:

APPLYING LOVE IN ACHIEVING
BALANCED PARENTING

Chapter One:
Time

A core predictor of which families produce children who grow up to be described as "*mentchen*" is the amount and quality of time spent by parents with their children. In a fascinating series of studies that have recently received media attention, researchers have found a direct correlation between the number of times a week parents eat dinner with their children and the latter's risk of abusing drugs. Families that eat dinner together once a week have children with lower risk for drug-abuse than those that never do. With each increasing night that parents and children eat together, drug abuse risk decreases to the point that there is virtually no risk for drug abuse in families in which parents and children eat dinner together every night.[1]

The importance of eating dinner together is not the eating or the dinner; it's the uninterrupted, focused interaction that seems to bear such valuable fruit. Children have sensitive radar and can tell whether their parents are really there and paying attention to them, or if their minds are preoccupied with concerns about work or other problems. Making time for your child entails truly being present both in mind and body, and providing the undivided attention that children need to develop and internalize proper values.

> *A father cleared his Sunday schedule to spend time alone with his 10-year-old daughter. His time with her was*

[1] Schwarzchild, M. (2000), "Alienated youth: help from families and schools," *Professional Psychology — Research & Practice, Vol. 31(1)*, pp. 95-96.

constantly interrupted by his cell phone ringing with business calls. After several hours of this, his daughter broke into tears and begged her father to go back to his office.

Recent studies have found that in addition to eating meals together, routine family "rituals" such as regularly scheduled family vacations, bedtime rituals, holiday and birthday celebrations are far more important to a child's healthy development than has been previously appreciated. This research has documented that children appear to benefit in a very powerful manner from partaking in regularly scheduled, structured and predictable activities. For example, studies indicate that families who value these activities and invest time and energy in insuring that children experience these rituals in a meaningful and predictable manner raise children who are less anxious, feel more loved and have more positive self-concepts.[2] Conversely, when these activities are disrupted because of traumatic family events such as divorce or chronic illness, children are at increased risk for a wide range of behavioral, academic and emotional difficulties.[3]

One of the most consistent research findings in the field of child abuse and neglect documents that children who are victims of neglect fare even worse than victims of child abuse. Harsh physical punishment of a child, while clearly harmful, at least shows that the parent cares enough to discipline the child. Such basic caring is often absent in families where a child is severely neglected. Of course, neglecting to spend time with one's children is a qualitatively different form of neglect than that seen in abusive families. Parents should keep in mind, however, that the damage that can attend neglecting our children because of our failure to prioritize spending time with them is often invisible. Although it may seem that a child has adjusted to being raised without strong input from his or her overtaxed parents, the long-term impact may not be evident for some time.

---

[2] Fiese, B. & Kline, C. (1993), "Development of the family ritual questionnaire," *Journal of Family Psychology,* pp. 290-299.

[3] Markson, S. & Fiese, B. (2000), "Family rituals as a protective factor for children with asthma," *Journal of Pediatric Psychology,* pp. 471-479.

Therapists and other professionals who work with children who have serious behavioral difficulties often comment that a major complaint voiced by these children is that their parents rarely seem to have time for them. We all realize that there are many factors that seemingly prevent parents from being able to spend as much time with their children as they would like. I (D.P.) was recently told that a child whose father was a lawyer who was working extremely long hours on a deal that kept him away from home for an unusual length of time — asked his mother in all seriousness, "Did Daddy die?" The enormous financial pressures imposed upon us by tuition bills and by the cost of supporting large families — coupled with frequent time consuming *simchos*, community and other social obligations — act as potent forces that prevent us from spending time with our children. In spite of the numerous forces competing for our time, it is important for parents to realize that the amount of time parents spend with their children when they are young is one of the most reliable predictors of how their children will turn out as adults. Once there is recognition that this is a priority of *paramount importance,* the ability to find the time will follow. On numerous occasions, parents who bring their children for counseling have told me that with an increase in the amount and quality of the time spent with their child (even if only during the time spent driving to and from the session), improved parent-child relationship and behavior often follow.

Certainly every parent wants to spend quality time with his or her children. As we all acknowledge, however, among the most common reasons why parents are unable to devote uninterrupted time and why children may become starved for parental attention is the tremendous financial pressures placed on parents. In many families, the effort to fulfill basic needs absorbs all of the energy and patience of the parents. It is important to realize, however, that once enough money is earned to meet these basic needs we must question our blind pursuit of earning as much money as possible. In a recent survey, people were asked what would improve the quality of their lives the most. The majority of respondents answered, "More money." Yet numerous studies have shown that these people are chasing an illusory goal. In fact, wealth is irrelevant to happiness. In what psychologists call the "principle of relative deprivation," people tend to evaluate their possessions not in terms of what they need to live in comfort but in comparison with those who have the most.[4] In living lives governed by this principle of "relative deprivation," we put ourselves on a treadmill on which the desire for more and more can never be satisfied.

> A 9-year-old girl was referred because she was caught stealing from her classmates, even though she came from an unusually wealthy family, where she was given whatever her heart desired. In counseling sessions she described feeling desperate to do anything to gain the attention of her workaholic father. Initially, the father resisted attempts to get him to spend more time with his daughter, claiming that he was working to insure that she had a proper inheritance. After the girl's behavior worsened, the father recognized that he needed to give his daughter the time that she craved. The girl's difficulties improved significantly thereafter.

Research indicates that it would be better if, when asked what would improve the quality of their lives the most, people would answer, "More time" to spend establishing connection to others, a sense of meaning in life and religious values. However, the more invested people become in material goals, the less sensitive they are to the rewards of time spent with their children. In spite of hectic schedules, making the finding of time with our children a front and center priority is one of the most important buffers against their developing a sense of alienation. If they do not build connections within the family they are at considerably greater risk for developing a sense of kinship with peers who may lead them astray.

◄ Jewish Perspectives on Time

Research in psychology has confirmed the essential role that control over one's time has on psychological and physical well-being. When individuals are deprived of such control they are at

---

[4] Myers, D. (2000), "The funds, friends, and faith of happy people," *American Psychologist*, Vol. 55, pp. 56-67.

risk for depression, anxiety and a variety of physical ailments. For example, the stress associated with working on a job which gives individuals little control over their schedules heightens risk for cardiovascular illness.[5] There is a saying, *Time will accomplish what intellect and thinking are not able to accomplish* (*Chut Ha'shani* 112,2).

This saying is particularly appropriate in the area of parenting. The most intellectually sophisticated and psychologically thought-out approach to parenting is meaningless if not implemented in the context of a parent-child relationship that makes spending time with the child a top priority.

The central role that Jewish thought puts on having control over one's time is illustrated in a commentary of the *Sforno* on the verse, *This month shall be for you* (*Exodus* 12:2).

What does the Torah mean by "This month is yours"? We are talking about the importance of control over one's time. The language of *to/for you* highlights the contrast between a free person's experience of time and that of a slave.

The *Sforno* explains:

"Henceforth, the months of the year shall be yours, to do with them as you desire. During the bondage, your days, your time, did not belong to you but was used to work for others and fulfill their will." A slave has no control or mastery over his time. He cannot sit down and make his own schedule. What is the essence of freedom? The freedom to control one's priorities, to choose to pursue what one's heart desires.

A corollary to this concept is illustrated later in this same weekly portion: *And you shall tell your son on that day, saying, "It is because of this that Hashem acted on my behalf when I left Egypt"* (*Exodus* 13:8).

A unique explanation is given as to what is being referred to by the word *this*. According to this interpretation *this* refers to the freedom that comes with being able to exercise our role as parents. Typically, slaves have been stripped of the right to have

[5] Helgeson V. (1992), "Moderators of the relation between perceived control and adjustment to chronic illness," *Journal of Personality and Social Psychology*, October, Vol. 63, No. 4, pp. 656-666.

control over any kind of family relationship. In contrast, at the *Seder*, we celebrate the freedom and responsibility that come with being able to educate our children. We explain to our children that for *this* — the freedom to engage in a dialogue between parents and children on the night of the *Seder* — we were liberated. The essence of self-determination is the freedom to invest our time in cultivating the parent-child relationship. Hashem liberated us to make this relationship possible. The true meaning of "*cheirus*" (freedom) is our ability, in contrast to slaves, to choose to transmit to our children the heritage of our people.

Our Sages in the *Mechilta* explain that when the Torah says: *Hashem saw our affliction, our travail (Deuteronomy 26:7)*, — it is referring to the toil involved in raising children. Similarly, in the special prayer recited when making a *siyum* marking the completion of a significant portion of the Torah we say: *We toil and they toil. We toil and receive a reward, they toil without receiving a reward.* The obvious question is that this flies in the face of logic. When a person works, doesn't he receive a paycheck to compensate him for his labor? The Chofetz Chaim explains that the meaning of the word *toil* refers to children, as we see from the *Haggadah*. What we are stressing at the *siyum* is how time is invested. Those who invest their time in their jobs or empty pursuits will reap no true reward. Similarly, if we do not take the time to transmit the proper values to our children and instead invest our time in empty activities, the result of the *toil* is often tension without reward. Alternatively, when hard work and time is invested in teaching children Torah and transmitting important values, then we have invested our time wisely in a manner that will reap reward.

The Kotzker Rebbe has a beautiful interpretation of the verse, *Like arrows in the hand of a warrior, so are the children of youth (Psalms 127:4)*, which poses the obvious question as to what connection exists between a warrior holding his bow and arrow and childhood. He explains that just as an archer's arrow will go further and straighter the closer he pulls the bow to himself, so too, the closer we hold our children to ourselves, the further and straighter they will go.

Recommendations:

- Make finding time with children a conscious and primary priority. In light of the truism that "the task expands to fill the time," parents are often pleasantly surprised how — once they commit themselves to carving out time from their hectic schedules — they are able to find time that they didn't know existed.

- Ritualize spending time alone with your child. If parents can find a way to systematically build in time alone with each of their children on a regular basis, they have a far greater likelihood that this will become part of the fabric of their lives. In large families, building in regular *individual* times with a child even only several times a month often has an impact far beyond what a parent thinks.

- Children know when parents are really attending to them or when a parent's mind is preoccupied with work problems or with reading the newspaper. When alone with your child make sure to shut out distractions. Shut off your cell phone and ask whoever is watching the other children to field phone messages or other intrusions.

- Establishing routines and family rituals that allow for shared time together are among the best guarantees that parents will routinely spend time with their children. Assigning children chores that can be done together with the parent can serve as a routine opportunity for interaction where both parent and child can share details of their day. Of course, asking children to help the parent prepare a meal or clean up after a meal has the added benefit of teaching them to share in family responsibilities.

- Parents should try to build in at least one shared enjoyable weekly activity with their children. Whether the activity is mundane like shopping, or more enjoyable, such as eating out, a trip to a museum, a concert, or a sports event, the activity itself is probably less important than the need to regularly schedule predictable together-times. Adolescents who may resist being seen on an outing with their parents may more easily tolerate engaging in more practical parent-child activities such as shopping. Keep in mind, however, that in spite of protestations to the contrary, even adolescents clearly benefit from spending time with their parents. A recent study found that the more time adolescents spent with their families, the higher their achievement test scores and the fewer their behavioral difficulties.[6]

■ Telling your child about *your* day can serve as an important model that should help your child reciprocate by sharing the details of *his* or *her* day. Keep in mind the research that suggests that parental knowledge of the details of their children's lives serves as an important protective buffer against later behavioral and emotional difficulties when their children reach adolescence.[7]

[6] Hofferth, S. L. & Sandberg, J. F. (2001), "How american children spend time," *Journal of Marriage and Family,* pp. 63, 295-308.

[7] Duncan, S. & Strycker, L. (2000), "Risk and protective factors influencing adolescent problem behavior," *Annals of Behavioral Medicine,* pp. 103-109.

Chapter Two:
Cultivating Uniqueness

The ability to accept and nurture the uniqueness in each of our children is at the core of effective parenting. A basic assumption guiding the work of marital therapists is the premise that when couples learn to truly accept their partners' personalities the relationships between husbands and wives improve. Psychologists have found that people can change only if they feel liked and accepted as they are. In the case of children, the need to be loved and understood is even greater. A pattern often seen in troubled children is a belief that they are different from the rest of their families and that they are not truly loved and accepted because of that difference. At a recent conference addressing the issue of "at-risk" children in the Orthodox community, a panel of children who were alienated from their families unanimously agreed that a central dynamic underlying this alienation was a feeling of being set apart from their families — either because of learning disabilities, behavior problems, or a mismatch between their temperament and that of their parents. They felt that they did not connect with their families or schools. These children ultimately found solace and a sense of belonging through companionship with similarly alienated peers.

A story is told about a child psychologist who married late in life. He said, "Before I had children I would write articles and give talks on child-rearing and always prefaced my remarks with a statement that I have five major theories about raising children.

That was when I had no children. Now I have five children and no theories." In a similar vein, a prominent child psychologist, who had his first child relatively late in life, told me (D.P.) that after seeing the reality of what raising children truly entailed, he wanted to call up his former patients to apologize. Until faced with the realities of raising children and, in particular, with the strong influence of temperament on child development, even a world-renowned expert did not fully appreciate the challenges of child-rearing. One of the most poignant insights that parents gradually arrive at after gaining firsthand experience with raising children is how powerful a role inborn temperament plays in shaping who a child will become. Although it is essential that parents take an active role in shaping those inborn characteristics, the basic "hardwiring" of temperament can be shaped, but not essentially changed.

A powerful lesson regarding the process of channeling a child's basic temperamental characteristics into productive areas is contained in the story of our Patriarch Abraham and the binding of Isaac on the altar *(Akeidas Yitzchak)*. If one of Abraham's core characteristics was the intensity of his beliefs, the test of his character came when he had to prove which of the two components of his personality he prioritized — ideology and *emunah* (faith) on the one hand, or the natural love of a father for his long-awaited son on the other.

How did Abraham find the strength of character to be willing to sacrifice his son? Ironically, the answer lies, in part, to what Abraham was exposed to while growing up. Terach, his father, also had a tremendous strength of belief. He took his iconoclastic son, Abraham, who according to the *Midrash* had smashed his father's idols, and brought him to King Nimrod to be executed. Terach's beliefs transcended the natural father-son bond. Abraham drew from that source in a similar manner, but he rechanneled this strength of character into service to God. Every parent has an area of strength that can be transmitted to his or her child in a manner that nurtures the child's uniqueness. The parent's role is to develop the positive aspects of a child's temperament in a manner that channels these traits in the proper direction.

Family therapists often ask a very telling series of questions when they are assessing a family: "What does it take to be a hero in your family?" "If your family had a bumper sticker that described the family's motto, what would it be?" For some families it might be, "Be a Torah scholar"; for others it might be, "Be kind." What if a child has a learning disability or an attention deficit that seriously hampers his ability to learn with diligence, and his family's bumper sticker reads, "Be a Torah scholar"? Even if he is a kind, considerate youngster, ever ready to do a favor and be of assistance to others, such a youngster is bound to feel that he is letting his family down — and this sense of failure permeates his childhood. If parents, however, can learn to value and nurture the positive inclinations of this child then he becomes transformed into a source of strength and pride to his parents.

> A 15-year-old boy, the son of a prominent rabbi, was referred after he was asked to leave his yeshivah because of oppositional behavior, such as questioning authority, and an aversion to learning. His parents were beside themselves with anger at their child, wondering why he couldn't be like his older brothers, who were widely admired for their ability to exemplify the family's bumper sticker, "Be a Torah scholar."
>
> The boy bitterly described feeling rejected by his family and yeshivah, and how he was increasingly attracted to a group of friends who were on the fringe of the community. The only family member to whom the child felt connected was his grandfather — a wealthy businessman, universally respected as a major supporter of numerous yeshivas. In a family session with the boy, his parents and his grandfather, the grandfather shared with his family what he was like at 15. He was the youngest of seven siblings of a prominent family living in Kovno in the years leading up to the Holocaust. His older brothers were admired as exemplary students in the local yeshivah. However, similar to his grandson, the grandfather was not a particularly stellar student. He had a strong belief, as the pre World War II situation deteriorated, that the family should escape to the United States. With tears in his eyes, pointing to his grandson, he told his daughter and son-in-law: "I was exactly like him. My parents and brothers thought I was being an alarmist and they begged me to abandon my

*obsessive insistence that the family leave Kovno." After
being convinced that his parents would not leave Europe,
he escaped to America on his own. He is the only member
of his family who survived. The grandfather turned to his
daughter and said, "Your son reminds me of myself when
I was his age — my questioning is the reason why your
family exists. Find a way to nurture his strengths."*

*This insight proved to be a turning point for the fam-
ily. They metaphorically expanded their family's bumper
sticker to include an admiration for the value of a spirited,
questioning child. The parents found their son a yeshivah
that was more attuned to his strengths and, although he
never achieved his brothers' prominence in learning, today
he is happily married and a successful businessman who is
a prominent supporter of numerous community charities.*

Research over the last half century has enhanced our understanding of the interaction between children's basic temperament
and "goodness of fit" with various styles of parenting.[1] From
infancy on, children have been found to differ in the following nine
dimensions, which comprise temperament:

1. Activity level.
2. Persistence (the ability to persevere in the face of obstacles).
3. Distractibility.
4. Response to novel situations or people (by approaching or
   withdrawing).
5. Adaptability (the ease of becoming accustomed to transitions).
6. Mood (positive or negative).
7. Intensity (of emotional expression).
8. Sensitivity (to sound, touch, light, etc).
9. Regularity (in patterns of eating, sleeping, etc.).

It is noteworthy that the concept of an inborn set of personality
traits is consistent with Maimonides' description of inborn personality predisposition in *Hilchos Dei'os* (*Sefer Mada, Hilchos
Dei'os,* Chapter One).

---

[1] Thomas A., Chess S. (1957), "An approach to the study of sources on individual difference in child behavior," *Journal of Clinical and Experimental Psychopathology
Quarterly Review of Psychiatry and Neurology,* 18:347-357.

Variations in temperament can be a source of difficulty or a source of strength. For example, children who have high-activity levels and low-frustration tolerance are more likely to have accidents around the house when they are preschoolers, and car accidents when they begin driving.[2] Children with anxious temperaments are more likely to respond intensely when the protective shield of family stability is disrupted by parental illness or divorce. They are also more likely to have difficulty with transitions, such as at the beginning of first grade, ninth grade, or when spending a year in Israel.

In contrast, there are numerous strengths associated with each temperament. When children with anxious temperaments are provided with a loving, stable environment they are more likely than their peers to grow up to be high achievers and leaders. The tendency of these children to connect strongly to others, to take work seriously and to be tuned in to the needs of friends and family members are assets that often make them more successful as adults than their non-anxious peers. I often wondered, however, what advantages there were to having a difficult disposition. What is the advantage to having a disregulated, intense and overly sensitive temperament? Several years ago this question was answered when researchers found that such children were more likely to survive a natural catastrophe. During a recent famine in Africa, infants with difficult temperaments had higher survival rates than their more easygoing peers, since their persistent and annoying cries attracted more care than those of the more placid infants.

> *A father was interviewed as part of his child's evaluation in a clinic for diagnosing attention-deficit disorder. The father explained that he too had been diagnosed as having this disorder as a child. He was hyperactive, impulsive and unmotivated in school. As he was growing up, his parents always compared him unfavorably to his three brothers who were exceptionally gifted students. When asked how things had turned out for him and his brothers, he*

[2] Gerra G., Avanzini, P., Zaimovic A. (1999), "Neurotransmitters, neuroendocrine correlates of sensation-seeking temperament in humans," *Neuropsychobiology,* 39:207-213.

answered that they were all exceptionally successful. As he explained, "One is a professor of physics at Harvard, one is a leading engineer on the faculty of M.I.T. and one is a respected oncology researcher at Stanford Medical School — and me? I support all of them." As an adult, this man's attention deficit turned from handicap to asset. He opened a car-repair center that was successful, but as is often the case with attention-deficit individuals, he quickly became bored and opened another center, followed by what ultimately became a widely admired and financially successful national chain.

Our teachers of ethical values have a very interesting insight into the blessing, *borei nefashos,* recited after eating vegetables, certain fruits, or drinking a beverage. This blessing ends with the words, *"boruch chai ha'olamim"* — "Blessed is He, the Life of the worlds." An obvious question arises. Why does this blessing refer to the world in a plural form? Typically, we refer to the world using the word *olam* in the singular, not *olamim* in the plural. The answer can be found at the beginning of the blessing: In the phrase, *borei nefashos rabbos v'chesronan,* God is referred to as the "Creator of numerous living things with their deficiencies." God built in limitations to every soul that was created. Every human being, no matter how gifted and well rounded, has, at least, some areas of relative deficit. There are Nobel laureates in physics who lack the skills and aptitude to be good farmers, and gifted physicians and lawyers who cannot change a light-bulb. Toward the end of the blessing we say, *l'hachayos bahem nefesh kol chai* — "with which to sustain the life of every being." This emphasizes the point that the uniqueness and the limitations of each individual provide the cement that binds society. This dynamic fuels an interdependence of all human beings in society. When parents face their child's areas of relative weakness, it is important to realize that just as God intended that every individual have areas of weakness and deficiency, this is part of a Divine plan that includes unique strengths, as well. What each individual will contribute to society cannot be duplicated by another.

Recent research on moral development in children has documented how children are more likely to internalize parental values if disciplinary strategies are tailored to the child's specific temperament. This series of studies has found that fearful children respond with high levels of anxiety even to situations that involve only the thought of wrongdoing. With these children, what works best is parental use of gentle discipline that de-emphasizes power and capitalizes on the child's natural sense of internal discomfort.[3]

In contrast, with temperamentally fearless children who do not readily respond with internal discomfort to transgressions, using a subtle approach will often not result in the child learning how to behave properly. An overly harsh approach, while tempting, has also not been found to be particularly effective. What seems to foster compliance best with impulsive and fearless children, researchers tell us, is many mutually positive interactions between parent and child in which the child feels loved and accepted for who he or she is. It is noteworthy that when psychologists design programs for defiant children, the first step recommended by most programs is to ask parents to increase the amount of enjoyable time they spend alone with their oppositional child. They are asked to spend twenty minutes a day alone with their difficult child, engaging in an activity which the child enjoys. During that time, no demands are made on the child and no questions are asked. Learning to enjoy the many strengths of a strong-willed child is an important ingredient in improving cooperation.[4]

Recognizing the unique educational needs of children is equally important. Some children have temperaments that are perfectly suited to a long school day; others find it difficult to remain still and focused for even short periods of time. Rabbi Samson Raphael Hirsch said (Genesis 25:27) that given Esau's hunter temperament, he should have been sent to a different school than his brother Jacob, who was by his very nature studious. One style

---

[3] Grusec, J & Goodnow, J. (1994), "Impact of parental discipline methods on the child's internalization of values — a reconceptualization of current points of view," Development Psychology, 30:4-19.

[4] Greene R. (1998), "The Explosive Child," New York: Harper Collins.

of education does not necessarily meet the needs of all children. One size does not fit all.

Rabbi Yisroel Salanter, the founder of the Ethical Values Movement in Judaism (*Mussar* Movement), made a similar point when he commented on the struggle that parents often have when trying to choose the best yeshivah for their child. He said that, in reality, if the Jewish community had the resources, we should establish a separate yeshivah for every student. Given the complexity of the unique needs of each child, no yeshivah can adequately cater to the strengths and weaknesses of each individual. Since it is not practical to do this, the role of the parent is magnified. It falls on every parent to assume the role, which by its very nature a school cannot assume: that of nurturing the uniqueness of each child.

There is a fascinating commentary by Rabbi Eliyahu of Vilna (the Vilna Gaon) on the famous verse in *Proverbs* (22:6), *Educate (train) the youth according to his way.* The Vilna Gaon says that if we don't take a child's nature into account when teaching him, he is in danger of not internalizing parental values. We can force a young child to act in a way not consistent with his nature when he is young, but once he grows old, says the Gaon, he will leave our teachings, because *"it is not possible to shatter a person's basic nature."*

This point is beautifully illustrated in a story about the Sage, the Alter of Slabodka, related in *Sefer Hamaros HaGedolim.* Two friends learning in Slabodka had very different temperaments. One learned nonstop in a focused and productive way, while the other wasted a lot of time and spent more time away from the yeshivah than in the halls of the *beis medrash.* For years, the Alter snubbed the studious young man while he lavished attention and praise on his far less studious friend. When the Alter paid a *shivah* visit (condolence call) to the studious man, the man bitterly asked the Alter why he had been treated so differently than his less-"deserving" friend for so many years. The Alter answered, "You find your place in learning, so when you come to me your intention is to satisfy your evil inclination by hearing praise from me. Attention from me at those times would be harmful. Your friend finds his place outside the walls of the yeshivah. When he comes to my house, his intention is to satisfy his good inclination by hearing words of Torah and ethical teaching. My job with him is to satisfy his spiritual interests." This epitomizes the kind of individualized approach that is necessary to help children maximize their potential.

Helping each of your children discover their uniqueness is at the heart of guiding them toward a life of meaning and happiness. Rabbi Akiva Tatz says the following on this topic.

> Real happiness is what you experience when you are doing what you should be doing. When you are moving clearly along your own road, your unique path to your unique destination, you experience real happiness. When you are moving along the path that leads to yourself, to the deep discovery of who you really are, when you are building the essence of your own personality and creating yourself, a deep happiness wells up within you. The journey does not cause happiness, the journey is the happiness itself (Rabbi Akiva Tatz, *The Thinking Jewish Teenager's Guide to Life* [Feldheim Publishers, 1999], p. 40).

Perhaps the greatest obstacle to helping children develop their unique strengths is when parents try to live through their children. Some parents view their children as an extension of themselves. A parent who wanted to achieve excellence in certain areas as a child, and could not, may feel that — through his children — he has another opportunity. Parents who feel guilt at being a disappointment to their own parents may in turn pressure their own children to achieve what they could not. While there is always an important role for parental guidance, ultimately, children must find their own way. No matter how painful, parents must realize that we often cannot save our children from making their own mistakes and finding their own path.

> A 12-year-old boy was referred because he was failing in school. The following history shed considerable light on why this was happening. The father was the son of Holocaust survivors who had spent their adolescence in the camps and, consequently, never went beyond an

elementary school education. They started a very success-
ful business after the war and their only wish was that
their son be happy. Higher education was not very impor-
tant to them, as they wanted to leave their business to him
and they saw no practical purpose in his getting secular
education past high school. He ended up living in a com-
munity of professionals. Although financially successful,
he had a chronic sense of inferiority because he was the
only member of his community who had not attended
college, let alone graduate school. This man swore to
himself that when he had children he would see to it that
they went to the finest colleges and graduate schools. No
matter what, he decided that his children would be pushed
to achieve academically so that they would not suffer the
humiliation he felt at being "uneducated." The mother in
this family came from a background where she and her
brother were pushed unbelievably hard to reach academic
perfection. One of her most vivid childhood memories was
when her brother brought home a very poor report card
and her mother responded by letting out a bloodcurdling
shriek and fainting. The academic pressure placed on her
by her parents was so unrelenting that she swore to herself
that, no matter what, when she had children she would
place absolutely no academic pressure on them. What was
most important was that her children be happy.

Not only was their son raised with mixed messages regarding
the importance of doing well in school, he was also the victim
of his parents' efforts to work out their own unresolved issues
through him. Instead of helping him discover his uniqueness,
his academic performance became the battleground over which
his parents tried to heal the wounds of their childhood.

Recommendations:

■ Parents cannot change their child's basic temperament. Rather, they need to adapt their approach to fit the child's unique needs.

■ Differences between children are not necessarily the result of a condition or disorder. Many parents feel responsible for, and guilty about having, a child whose temperament sets them apart from other children. They are relieved to know that their child is normal and that they are not to blame for causing the child's difficulties. It is important to differentiate between the child who *can't* and the one who *won't*. Parents often lose their patience with a child whose behavior seems willful, when, in fact, he is acting that way because it is who he is. For example, an intense child who is overly loud when upset should not be punished for acting that way any more than he should be punished for being loud when he is happy.

■ Understanding a child's temperament is not the same as not holding the child accountable for his misbehavior. For example, the fearless children discussed earlier actually need *more* structure and limits than the even-tempered children. Research on these children concludes that because they are more likely to act without thinking, they respond best when rules and instructions are concise, clearly spelled out and brief. Parents cannot rely on unprompted recollection of rules as they would with children with more easygoing temperaments. In addition, consequences (both rewards and punishments) must be delivered without delay and far more systematically than is the case with other children. Since these children become bored easily, parents should recognize that if they are using rewards to motivate them, the shelf life of most rewards is, at the most, three weeks. New rewards should be thought of after this period of time in order to recapture the child's interest and excitement.

■ As noted earlier, a whole different style is needed for dealing with fearful children. Research shows that children who fall into this category do best if their parents gently push them to confront their fears. It is important, however, to find the most effective window of comfort. Pushing too hard, so that the child is overwhelmed by his or her fears, tends to make things worse. Pushing too little carries the danger that the child will fall prey to his or her fears and not learn to conquer them. What tends to work best is a gradual approach that continuously challenges fearful children to push themselves to confront their fears. As they gain mastery over what was previously overwhelming, they gain the motivation and strength to reach a little higher.

- The rigid child has been described as a child who is inflexible, irritable, a perfectionist and intolerant of even minor change in routine. These children can be particularly trying to parents, who should strive to develop a parenting style that tries to anticipate situations that may serve to trigger temper outbursts. In dealing with such children, parents are often called upon to summon up reserves of patience and calmness, particularly during times of transition and change (e.g. the beginning of the school year, vacations and family transitions). Many children with this temperament are sensitive to overstimulation. For example, a moderately raised voice used by parents in disciplining such a child can be experienced by him or her as intensely as an average person might respond to the sound of fingernails scratching a blackboard. Consequently, a particularly calm approach needs to be used in parenting the rigid child, who can even experience overly enthusiastic praise as upsetting.

  In dealing with the perfectionist tendencies of these children it is important for parents to recognize that in areas such as learning, academics, or sports, rigid children might prefer not trying rather than try and risk failure. The goal is to achieve a balance between calmly but firmly encouraging them to risk new challenges and empathically understanding how difficult this might be for them.

- Parents of fearful children tend to have similar styles themselves. They may unwittingly exacerbate their children's difficulties in this area by placing excessive emphasis on how their children appear to others. They may also unwittingly feed fearful withdrawal from anxiety-provoking social situations by discouraging visits of friends and keeping themselves and their children away from anxiety-inducing social events. Parents who push themselves and confront their own anxieties can have a positive effect on their fearful child as well.

- In dealing with sibling rivalry, keep in mind that children should be dealt with not equally, but according to their unique needs. It is not at all uncommon for me to see large families where all of the children have the same bedtime — even though there is a wide age span between the oldest and youngest. Parents usually explain that they do not want to deal with crying younger children who are upset that they have to go to bed earlier than their older siblings. However, this approach is not fair to the needs of the older children. In general, as long as children feel that a parent is being fair, they will generally understand if one sibling is treated differently than another.

Chapter Three:
Motivating Children

C hildren are born with a natural drive for competence and mastery. They are internally motivated to take satisfaction in the challenges provided by learning, play and exploration. Some children retain a strong drive to excel and continue learning with little prodding by teachers or parents. They have a strong desire to master challenging tasks and they revel in the feeling of mastery and competence that accompanies learning. On the other hand, there are other children, even in the early grades, who seem to have lost this internally driven motivation. Among the forces that contribute to the derailment of the early drive for mastery is the child's acquired belief that he cannot do what is asked of him. While the factors that foster such an acquired belief vary with each child, certain kinds of issues tend to contribute to a child's development of these feelings of inadequacy. In some children, learning disabilities that are not diagnosed and addressed can give them deep-seated senses of inadequacy relative to their peers. In other cases, external stress, such as living in homes with chronic financial stress or marital conflict, is the culprit. These children can become too preoccupied to concentrate.

Perhaps the most frequent force behind the squelching of a child's natural desire to learn can be traced to parents or teachers who set unrealistic standards for the child's performance in light of that particular child's ability or temperament. They convey their disappointment — through criticism or otherwise — regarding the child's inability to meet these unrealistic standards. In all of these instances, when a child repeatedly experiences failure, he learns to give up on himself. He suppresses his inner drive for competence rather than risk facing painful feelings of frustration and inadequacy.

In order to study the connection between parenting and academic motivation, psychologists look at children's responses when asked to complete unsolvable puzzles in the presence of their mothers. Some children rise to the challenge. They respond to this impossible task by becoming energized rather than frustrated. When faced with their inability to complete the puzzle, these children redouble their efforts. In spite of their failure, these children maintain high expectations for future success. On the other hand, another group of children exhibits a pattern characterized by pervasive helplessness. They become easily discouraged and irritable in the face of the difficult puzzles. They attribute their failure to forces over which they have no control and are pessimistic about their chances of solving similar puzzles in the future. What differences in parenting styles account for this disparity?

When faced with statements such as, "I can't do it," mothers of the highly motivated children respond not only with reassurance conveying belief in their children's abilities, but also with suggestions for trying a different approach. The children's attention is shifted away from feelings of inadequacy and back toward mastering the task. In contrast, the mothers of the unmotivated children make critical comments about their children's competence. When these children made statements reflecting their belief that they could not complete the puzzles, the mothers of the unmotivated children typically responded with a suggestion that the children quit or move on to the next puzzle, rather than giving the children encouragement.

As discussed earlier, an overly punitive approach is not an effective method of motivating children. On the other hand, parents assume that a reward system is a beneficial way to motivate children. What is surprising to many parents is the potentially debilitating effect that the use of rewards can have on children's motivation. A recent statistical analysis of over 100 studies examined the effect of rewards on children's inner motivation to complete a task. The surprising consensus of these studies was that tangible rewards, such as money or stickers, significantly undermined a child's natural drive to succeed. Rewards may result in temporary improvements, but once they stop, children typically become unmotivated. They develop an externally driven attitude with regard to learning that is predicated on a "What do I get for doing this?" approach.

This same body of research found a number of other intriguing findings about the connection between rewards and motivation. When children are told that they will be given a reward for completing a task, they find the task less interesting than tasks for which they were given no material rewards. Rewards also affect the amount of effort children choose to invest in learning. Numerous studies have found that, when faced with an array of possible tasks, rewarded children tend to pick the easiest. In contrast, when not given rewards, children faced with a variety of challenging tasks tend to pick tasks that are just beyond their current level of ability. Perhaps of greatest concern is the finding that children who come from families that rely heavily on material rewards tend to be less generous than those reared in families that help motivate their children by teaching them to tap into their inner resources. It is not surprising that parents who teach children to focus on the material benefits of performing raise children who place great value on the material at the expense of developing the inner strength and empathy that are the building blocks of generosity.

The reward-motivation connection is not only applicable in academic areas. A widely quoted study yields interesting insights regarding the use of rewards to get children to eat certain foods. In this study, preschoolers were introduced to a new beverage and divided into three groups. The children in the first group were only asked to drink the beverage. No pressure of any kind was put on them. A second group was given lavish praise for drinking the beverage, and a third group was given treats for drinking. Initially the children who were praised or received treats drank more then the nonrewarded children. Over time, however, a very intriguing shift took place. Both groups of rewarded children came to dislike the drink. The children who had received no rewards liked the drink as much or more than they had earlier. While on the surface, this finding seems surprising, many parents already recognize that the more pressured a child feels, the more he resists our efforts to get him to comply.

If punitive approaches and tangible rewards hamper a child's motivation, how can children be properly motivated? Research shows that, as in other areas of parenting, the answer is very complex. Time, love, support and a nurturing of a child's unique abilities are among the key ingredients. Psychologists have identified the following essential components in parent-child relationships that foster motivated children:

1. Parenting practices that are geared toward helping a child experience success and failure **not** as reward and punishment, but as feedback and information. Academic success is associated with a parental style that (a) conveys faith in the child's abilities, (b) fails to take over for the child and (c) uses questions and explanations to teach or challenge. In contrast, when parents take over for their child, motivation is suppressed.

2. Use of praise and encouragement in a context that conveys to the child that the parent believes he or she is competent. Such praise needs to be delivered in a manner that is perceived by the child as sincere and not coming from a parent's attempt to control him or her. A child's belief in his or her ability, his or her academic self-concept, is perhaps the main contributor to academic success or failure. Researchers have found that the most powerful predictor of this sense of competence is parental confidence in the child. Parents who do not believe in their child's potential tend to have children who display helpless behaviors in the face of challenging academic tasks, and are more likely to be viewed as unmotivated by their teachers.

3. The more children believe that there is a connection between their efforts and successful outcomes, the more motivated they become. For example, studies have found that academically successful children are those who have a good understanding of what

parents and teachers expect of them and what it takes to succeed in school.

4. Academic motivation is directly related to the extent to which parents encourage their children to make their own choices. Studies indicate that when children are offered choices regarding some component of their schoolwork, they show more enjoyment, better performance and greater persistence then when they are given no choice.

The importance of motivating children by recognizing their unique potential is beautifully illustrated in a Talmudic passage in *Berachos* (48a): *Abaye and Rava [when boys] were once sitting in the presence of Rabbah. Rabbah asked them, "To Whom do we address blessings?" They answered, "To Hashem." "And where does Hashem live?" Rava pointed to the ceiling. Abaye went outside and pointed to the sky. Rabbah said to them, "Both of you will grow up to become great men." As the popular saying goes, 'Small pumpkins are discernible when they burst forth from their sap.'*

Both of these *Amoraim* would grow up to become leaders of their generation, building on the seeds of their personalities that were already evident when they were young children. Rava, who used his imagination, pointed to the roof and imagined what was in the heavens. He could remain inside and still answer the question, "To Whom do we address blessings?" He did not need to have the answer directly in front of him. Once his "stalk" was nurtured, Rava was able to develop and build his legacy based on creative, independent reasoning. Abaye answered the question by pointing to the actual sky; an answer that is consistent with his later approach to learning and Torah, embodied by a reliance on transmitted knowledge rather than on creative thought. What if, instead of Rabbah — their rebbi who reveled in and recognized their unique strengths — the future leaders had had a teacher who suppressed their differences? What would have happened had Abaye been punished for leaving class to go outside? What would have become of Rava's potential had his creative responses not been nourished?

The *Yalkut Shimoni* offers a similar lesson about the ingredients of motivation. Rava, the beneficiary of a rebbi who appreciated his uniqueness, says, "*A person should always learn Torah from somebody who he wants [to learn from]*"... Rebbe says, "*He should always learn what his heart desires*" (Yalkut Shimoni, *Psalms* Ch. 1).

An essential ingredient in motivating students is having a rebbi or teacher whom the child likes *(from somebody who he wants)*. The key to a child's liking a teacher is often whether the child senses that the teacher likes and appreciates him or her. I often see children who are referred for repeated academic failure. When I obtain a detailed history of their performance in school, I hear of repeated difficulties punctuated by certain subjects or years in which the child does unexpectedly well. Almost without fail, these children will tell me that they did well that year or in that class because they had a rebbi or teacher who really liked them. These teachers are fondly remembered as appreciating the child unconditionally. Such educators do not take a child's academic inadequacies or misbehavior personally. They accept the child, flaws included, and they nourish each child's unique strength.

The second part of the *Yalkut Shimoni* refers to *what* he learns, the content *(what his heart desires)*. Another important ingredient in motivating children is leaving room for them to delve into and excel in subject matter that they really enjoy learning. An exclusive focus on one subject or one type of intelligence robs children who are gifted in areas other than subjects such as Talmud (that form a school's core curriculum), of the chance to excel and feel accomplished. Giving children an opportunity to develop in a specific area of strength tends to have a positive spillover effect to other subjects as well.

> *A 13-year-old boy was referred for disruptive behavior in school. He, the class clown, was frequently asked to leave class for calling out, getting out of his seat and generally disrespectful behavior toward his teachers. What ultimately led to his suspension from school and the referral for counseling was when he was caught stealing money from a teacher. He used the stolen money to buy candy for friends.*

Psychological testing determined that the boy had an undiagnosed learning disability that particularly impacted on his ability to learn Talmud — the focus of the major part of his day in yeshivah. It was also determined that he had remarkable artistic and musical skills. The school was very receptive to tapping into the boy's strengths. As a result, his widely admired posters and paintings advertised upcoming school events and he was a featured musician at the school dinner. This recognition, coupled with a modification of his learning schedule to accommodate his learning disability, effected a significant improvement in the boy's behavior and motivation.

◀§ Indirect Approaches to Motivation

Rabbi Michel Twersky, who built a vibrant Jewish community in Milwaukee, advised a group of rabbis about the key component that he viewed as central to his success in motivating the religious growth of others. "As long as I had a conscious agenda of trying to make people more religious I failed. It was only when I wasn't trying, when all I cared about was building relationships, with no strings attached, that others became motivated to grow spiritually." This dynamic informs us of an essential ingredient in motivating children. They, too, are most powerfully motivated through indirect methods. Parents must appreciate the importance of a relaxed nonthreatening atmosphere in the home when discipline is being imposed. Discipline, yes; fear, no.

This concept is well illustrated in the following Talmudic passage: *Rabbah used to say something humorous to his scholars before he began teaching in order to amuse them; after that he sat in an atmosphere of trepidation and began his lecture* (*Pesachim* 117a). Expanding on this the *Yalkut Shimoni* says, *The humorous comment said at the beginning of his class served to "open the hearts" of the students* (*Yalkut Shimoni, II Kings* Ch. 3).

The role of humor in motivating children is echoed in recent research that has lent empirical support to Rabbah's approach. For example, educational psychologists have found that humor enhances memory.[1] Furthermore, in the spirit of *from somebody who he wants,* surveys have found that children describe humor and a joy-filled approach to learning as among the most cherished attributes of adults they admire.[2] Humor has also been identified as a core component of resilience in coping with stressful situations. For example, research indicates humor to be among the most potent coping mechanisms used by families dealing with life-threatening illnesses in their children.[3]

The power of the humor/joy-filled approach as a source of academic motivation is illustrated by the following vignette:

> *I (DP) was visiting a small town in the center of the United States, where a number of chassidim work in the local kosher slaughterhouse. Their children attend the town's yeshivah, where the curriculum has an exclusive focus on Jewish studies. Although there is virtually no formal secular education, the state requires that the students take a yearly achievement test. By coincidence, I was visiting the principal of the yeshivah when he received the results of that year's state tests. I was surprised to see that virtually all students had received scores that placed them towards the top of academic achievement relative to their public school peers who spent their entire school day receiving formal secular instruction. When I asked the principal how, in the absence of formal instruction, he accounted for his students' mathematics and reading excellence he invited me to join him later that day to observe what the yeshivah students do during their leisure time. That evening the principal took me to a basement of one of the families in town. The children were gathered around a bank of computers enthusiastically playing various mathematical, reading comprehension and other educational computer games.*

---

[1] Schmidt, S., "Effects of humor on sentence memory," *Journal of Experimental Psychology, Learning, Memory and Cognition,* 1994, 20:4, 953-967.

[2] Taffel R., *Nurturing Good Children Now,* St. Martin's Press, 2000.

[3] Wade, S.L.; Borawski, E.A.; Taylor, H.G.; Drotar, D; Yeates, KD; Stanun, T.; "The relationship of caregiver coping to family outcomes during the initial year following pediatric injury," *Journal of Consulting and Clinical Psychology,* 2001, 69:3, 406-416.

The principal explained that in keeping with chassidic practice, the children were not allowed to watch television or movies. One of the only "fun" activities available to them was playing the educational computer games. Apparently this indirect form of self-education was enough to place them at the top of their state's achievement scores.

In a fascinating study, a group of psychologists compared geometric reasoning in a group of Israeli students attending ultra-Orthodox (*charedi*) schools with that of peers attending mainstream schools. The students in the secular schools had received extensive formal instruction in mathematics and science while those in the *charedi* schools received almost none. Contrary to expectations, the *charedi* 12- to 14-year-olds solved the tests of geometric reasoning problems more often than did their secular peers who had received extensive instruction in the subject.[4]

There are a number of possible factors to explain the counterintuitive finding of this study. The researchers hypothesize that yeshivah students benefit from an educational system that values the inclusion of the perspective of others, closely reasoned arguments, depth of understanding and the interactive process of studying in *chavrusahs* (dyads), rather than the teacher-controlled learning approach that dominates secular schools. It is of note that the yeshivah students in this study spent significantly more time than their secular peers in trying to solve the geometry problems. It is possible that in contrast to the secular students, the geometry problem-solving process was viewed as a "fun" challenge rather than one more test of their mathematical knowledge.

The connection between one's emotional state and intellectual motivation and productivity is further illustrated by the following discussion in the Talmud: *"To David, a psalm" intimates that the Shechinah [the Holy Presence] rested upon him and then he uttered [that] song; "A psalm of David" intimates that he [first] uttered [that particular] psalm and then the Shechinah rested upon him. This teaches you that the Shechinah rests [upon*

---

[4] Dembo, Y, Levin, I and Siegler, R., "A comparison of the geometric reasoning of students attending israeli ultra-Orthodox and mainstream schools," *Developmental Psychology*, January 1997, Vol. 33, No. 1, 92-103.

man] neither in indolence nor in gloom, nor in frivolity, nor in levity, nor in vain pursuits, but only in rejoicing connected with a religious act, for it is said, "And now bring me a musician. And it happened that as the musician played, the hand of Hashem came upon him" (Pesachim 117a).

The Talmud in *Pesachim* is speaking of the connection between a joyful state of mind and creativity. In discussing the difference between those chapters of *Psalms* that begin with "To David, a psalm" versus those with the reversed introduction "A psalm to David," the Talmud tells us that when King David was in a state of joy and happiness he was inspired to compose a particular psalm that began "To David, a psalm," implying that the song started with him — his inner joy served as his motivation to compose. In contrast, when King David was depressed he could not be self-motivated; the process was then reversed. "A psalm to David" initiates those psalms, and it is the *song* that puts King David in the proper state of mind.

A well-known psychologist has done extensive research documenting what he has found to be a key ingredient in happiness and creativity. "Flow" is a psychological term used to describe an experience that is so engrossing and enjoyable that it becomes worth doing for its own sake, even though it may have no consequence outside itself. This experience is what takes place when one is thoroughly involved in something that is enjoyable and meaningful. Research on "flow"[5] has found that peak levels of creativity, productivity and happiness are most likely to emerge when an individual is able to work in a manner that relates to the task at hand without competing emotional pressures. Applied to the setting of fostering motivation in children, parents should be aware that "flow" is most likely to flourish in an atmosphere that allows the child to work or study without the external pressure of parents or teachers, or the internal pressures of feelings of inadequacy, anger, or conceit.

This concept is beautifully illustrated in what our Rabbis teach us about the verse cited earlier from the Talmud in *Pesachim*.

---

[5] Csikszentmihalyi, M., "If we are so rich, why aren't we happy?", *American Psychologist,* October 1999, Vol. 54, No. 10, 821-827.

The Talmud illustrates the power of happiness and song to instill productivity by giving the example of Elisha who recognized that the best strategy for transcending his sadness and anger (*Rashi, Pesachim* 66b) was through the indirect method of using music to make him receptive to the word of Hashem.

The Talmud quotes Elisha in *II Kings* 3:15: *And now, bring me a musician. And it happened that as the musician played, the hand of Hashem came upon him.*

The simple meaning is that since Elisha was upset he was not receptive to the message of Hashem. The music lifted his spirits which, in turn, put him into the proper frame of mind to receive God's message. The wording, however, is awkward. The verse could have told us that the music had its desired effect on Elisha. Why is the seemingly redundant phrase *as the musician played* inserted, referring to the action of playing the music and not the effect it had on Elisha? The Kotzker Rebbe explains that this added phrase teaches us an important lesson. Even the finest musician cannot succeed in bringing forth the proper music from an instrument unless the musician is one with the instrument. Even the most talented musician will not actualize his musical gift if he approaches his music with an attitude clouded by egotism and self-involvement. A musician who thinks as he plays, *Look how talented I am,* never achieves greatness. It is only when the musician has no personal emotions — just as the instrument has no feelings — that true genius emerges.

Of course, as with all areas of parenting, a balance between love and limits is essential. In the area of motivating children, limit-setting is as important as nurturing internal motivation. This balance is reflected in the Talmud in the tractate *Kesubos: Rav Yitzchak said, [The Sages] enacted in Usha that a man should bear with his [recalcitrant] son until he is 12 years old (Kesubos* 50a).

The Talmud explains that up to a certain age (the actual age is subject to debate in the Talmud), a parent should accommodate his child, i.e. show patience and flexibility in studying with him. Afterward, the Talmud describes the necessity of shifting to increasing demands and expectations. In the words of the Talmud, *stuff him like an ox.* This means that the curriculum should be increased, as well as the demands placed on the older child, by requiring that he study as much as he can absorb.

Fostering an atmosphere in the home that strikes a balance between expectations and limit-setting on the one hand and an atmosphere conducive to harnessing the child's inner drive to achieve on the other, not only maximizes the child's motivation to achieve, but also nurtures an equally lofty goal — the development of an integrated personality. The word *personality* has as its root the Latin word *persona*, which means *mask*. Children who are pressured to perform to fulfill their parents' needs rather than develop their inner strengths are at risk of relating to others only by donning a mask that they think others want of them. These children risk developing a fragmented personality that is not driven by an internal moral compass.

The Talmud teaches us that Rav Yosef would spare no expense in celebrating Shavuos, the holiday that commemorates our receiving the Torah: *On Shavuos, Rav Joseph would say to his servants, "Prepare me a third-born calf (a choice delicacy)," saying, "But for the influence of this day, [causing me to learn Torah], how many 'Yosefs' are there in the marketplace!"* (Pesachim 68b).

The teachers of ethical values cite this Talmudic passage as teaching us a very important lesson in the integration of personality. Rav Yosef was saying, "If it were not for the integrating power of Torah I would not be just one Yosef, I would be multiple Yosefs. Like so many others, I would lead a fragmented life characterized by my wearing the numerous masks elicited by varied surroundings. Thanks to the unifying force of Torah I am complete, a person of integrity. I am an integrated personality." The Torah imparts a specific life philosophy that instills clarity, consistency and integrity. Transmitting this philosophy to children allows their uniqueness to emerge. This is the ultimate goal, since once a child is provided an atmosphere that allows him to become one with the Torah, once he is allowed to not be just another Yosef in the street, then the challenge of how to motivate him becomes irrelevant. His intrinsic motivation will fuel a natural thirst to develop a genuine, integrated and unique personality.

Recommendations:

- Praise that is well earned and specific can be a powerful motivator for a child. Instead of general praise such as, "You did well on that test," parents should be more specific about the reasons for the praise. Comments such as, "I know how much you studied," or "Look at how well you answered that difficult question," are more effective motivators. Some parents undermine their attempts at reinforcing a child's good behavior by ending a compliment with criticism. "Your room is so clean, why can't you always keep it this way?" The net effect of concluding a compliment with a negative statement is to leave the child feeling criticized and unmotivated.

- In motivating children it is important to make judicious use of reprimands. Reprimands are most effective when they are brief and unemotional. Nagging via repetitive reminders to study tends to undermine motivation. Contrary to popular belief, repetition does not make a request sink in. Instead, agree on a time to discuss your concerns. After making sure that you will not be interrupted (e.g. phone off the hook, siblings out of the way), state briefly and calmly what you want to discuss. Parents should initially ask their child what they think will improve their performance in school. Feelings of frustration or anger on the part of the child should be acknowledged and validated. Parents are often surprised that a collaborative approach with their child can generate ideas that adults had not thought of. Ask your child what he thinks will make his experience in school better. Write down his suggestions and agree on a plan for implementing them.

- Parents should think of their role in motivating children to do homework as that of a consultant rather than manager. In the workplace the role of a consultant is to be available without hovering or managing. Parents should strive for this kind of distance, and only offer help at the child's request. This maximizes the chances that the child will learn to work independently and, ultimately, truly own the responsibility for schoolwork. Examples of appropriate parental involvement in homework include assisting a child who is unable to proceed further, who wants his or her work checked, or who wants to be tested. Parents should also do their best to make sure that the child is working in a room that is well lit and has a dedicated work area. Homework time should be scheduled and respected no differently than other appointments that the child might have. An evaluation by a learning or mental health specialist should be considered if parents find their child to be so distracted or disorganized that he or she is unable to complete homework unless a parent is constantly present.

■ Although common sense dictates that a child should work without distractions, research suggests that, in some cases, children learn better when allowed to study while listening to music in the background. Of course, one size does not fit all — some children learn better under completely quiet conditions. The most logical way of determining what is optimal for your child is to experiment with having him or her do homework of similar levels of difficulty with and without background music.

■ In some cases failure to work in school may reflect underlying feelings of depression. If a child seems apathetic, inattentive, irritable and/or unable to enjoy himself, parents should consult a mental health professional to determine if these symptoms reflect a depressive disorder that requires professional attention. This is particularly the case if the above symptoms also dominate in nonschool-related areas as well.

■ As a general rule of thumb, if an adolescent's grades are above 85-90, parents can safely let the logical consequences set up by the school take over when a child does not seem to be taking responsibility to study or complete homework assignments seriously enough. If an adolescent, who has strong academic potential, is performing significantly below his or her abilities because of poor study habits, it is appropriate for parents to take a strong stance by insisting on a parentally supervised study time during which the child is not allowed to engage in any leisure activities. It is important that the parents not get involved in the quality of the adolescent's work unless asked for help or feedback.

■ A warm relationship with parents is one of the most potent motivators of religious and academic development. When parents learn Torah with their child it is essential that the emotional atmosphere be dominated by a warm and loving interaction. Rabbi Shimon Russell, a Lakewood, New Jersey expert in parent-adolescent relationships, recommends that parents have individual learning sessions with their children at least once a week. The exclusive focus of these sessions should be on looking for something to praise. It stands to reason that, if the goal of parents is to instill a love of Torah in their children, the warm feelings associated with these sessions are far more important than whatever material is taught in a pressured or critical interaction.

Chapter Four:
Instilling Values

C hildren are not born with a natural sense of what is right and what is wrong. Transmitting values takes effort, thought and an awareness of what standards we want to set (and impart) for respectful and proper behavior in our children. Among the most basic values that parents must instill in their children is gratitude (*hakaras ha'tov*). In fact, gratefulness is such a central value of Judaism that the very name *Yehudi*, "Jew," has as its source the Hebrew word *hodaah*, thankfulness. Regarding the birth of Leah's fourth child, the Torah teaches us that *She conceived again, and bore a son and declared, "This time let me gratefully praise Hashem"; therefore she called his name Judah; then she stopped giving birth (Genesis* 29:35).

Rashi explains: "I took more than my share so I must be thankful." Leah knew through prophecy that Jacob would have twelve sons. As one of four wives, her fair share would have been three sons. The verse, "This time let me gratefully praise Hashem," reflects Leah's recognition that she received more than her portion. This is why Jews are called *Yehudim* — to be Jewish is to express gratitude.

Yet many children take for granted what their parents do for them. They are not even aware of the debt of gratitude that they owe to their parents. In turn, parents are often uncomfortable with asking for recognition for the countless acts of kindness they do for their children. Instilling in children the habit of thanking their parents is an important component of teaching them this central value of being a Jew.

Another component that parents should attend to in the moral education of their children is the lesson that children should be helpful and considerate. They should pitch in and help out with the family's everyday chores and tasks. Once upon a time, a universal requirement of children was to be helpful and share in family chores and responsibilities. Today, this makes some parents uncomfortable. Interesting insights on the benefits of requiring children to assume their fair share in helping with family chores comes from research into what factors are associated with children who are successfully raised in families facing chronic hardships such as poverty or violence. Children who are required to help out and take an active role in assisting their parents face adversity are more resilient and better adjusted as adults than children who are not required to play this active role. Requiring active contributions by children gives them a sense of mastery and control and teaches them to go beyond their own selfish needs.

In addition to *directly* teaching our children what is expected of them, the transmission of proper values is often a subtle process. It is important to be aware of the many indirect forces that shape our children's values, since raising a *mentch* is so much more complicated than only telling a child what to do. Longitudinal studies that identify the core ingredients associated with raising an empathic child identify a subtle process that is typically present in such families. Parents who raise children who are kind and charitable as adults expose them to discussions that show respect for those with whom they disagree. Imagine a family sitting around a Shabbos table discussing an issue about which they feel passionately. Parents who show contempt or disrespect regarding those with whom they disagree are conveying a very powerful message to their children. They are modeling an approach to conflict that includes disdain and contempt for those who view the world differently. Whether the discussion is about family members, friends, or the leadership of the local shul or yeshivah, showing respect for those with whom we disagree is a very powerful lesson for children. A crucial facet of this process is parental promotion of perspective-taking in their children. It is common sense that when children are encouraged to see things respectfully through the eyes of others — even those with whom we disagree — they are getting an important lesson in one of the basic building blocks of empathy. Parents whose discussion style is associated with instilling the proper values in their children are also more likely to actively encourage their children's participation in family discussions. These parents draw their children into discussions with adults and supportively challenge their children's thinking in an atmosphere that is marked by respect and tolerance for the views of others, as well as that of their children.

> After I gave a lecture that included a discussion about the importance of showing respect to others in conversations we have in front of our children, a rabbi in the audience told me the following story. He had just taken a position as the leader of a shul that had had a rocky relationship with the previous rabbi. He was shocked to hear that the son of one of his congregants had just become engaged to a non-Jewish girl. He met with the young man to try to understand how this happened and to attempt to dissuade him from his decision to intermarry. The young man explained that, all of his life, the conversations he heard around the Shabbos table were dominated by his parents' bitterly complaining about the previous rabbi. When company came over, this, too, was a major topic of conversation. He asked the rabbi, "How do you expect me to view this religion? I was a young, impressionable boy and my view of Judaism was mainly informed by the bitter anger my parents and their friends felt toward their spiritual leader. I see no reason to continue to belong to a religion that was so devalued by my parents and their friends."

Another indirect force that shapes a child's acquisition of the proper values is having an actively involved father. The role of mothers in shaping a child's moral development is obvious. Less intuitive is the finding in a number of research studies that active involvement of fathers in their young children's moral education is the strongest predictor of their children's moral reasoning and empathy in adolescence and young adulthood. Conversely, in homes with absentee fathers, children are at increased risk for behavioral difficulties. This finding is in keeping with what we are taught in *Proverbs* 1:8: *Hear, my child, the discipline of your father, and do not forsake the teaching of your mother.* King Solomon is telling us that when it comes to *mussar* — the limit-setting component of parenting — fathers play a particularly central role. Although there are many forces that may be pulling a father away from active involvement with his children, it is important for him to remember that, especially when his children are young, he has a pivotal role to play in their moral development. Young children living in homes where their fathers are largely absent experience what psychologists call *father hunger*. They have an almost physical thirst for active interaction with their father. Once children reach adolescence, they have much less interest in spending time with either parent than they did when they were younger. While a father continues to play a central role in shaping his child's values into adulthood, he needs to actively prioritize his role as moral educator of his young child during the critical window of opportunity that fades all too quickly.

Research in neuropsychology has uncovered two types of learning that are part of the moral education process. Didactic learning, for example, teaching a child *Hilchos Derech Eretz* (the laws of proper conduct) predominantly involves the brain's left hemisphere. When the left side of the brain dominates, learning consists of logical, factual thinking. This type of learning is characterized by abstract, context-independent ideas. Right-hemisphere learning consists primarily of concrete human and interpersonal situations. The focus of this part of the brain is on people and the cause of their actions.

Right-hemisphere learning is what takes place when children learn through stories or by absorbing the moral behavior they see in admired adults. Such learning is integrated in a more pervasive way than its more scientific, left-hemisphere counterpart. It becomes part of the person, rather than disconnected pieces of knowledge. Although parents may be concerned that stories or *chessed* (acts of kindness) projects take their children away from *real* learning, *softer* approaches such as telling stories that contain moral lessons or affording children opportunities to perform *chessed* are the most powerful methods we have for effectively transmitting our values to our children.

The powerful impact of role models on the behavior pattern of the child is perhaps the most potent type of right-hemisphere learning. Seeing *tzaddikim* (righteous people) in action helps our children internalize proper values in a particularly meaningful manner, as the verse (*Isaiah* 30:20) teaches us, *And your eyes will behold your teacher* . According to the *Radak,* a Scriptural commentator, this teaches us how important "seeing" a teacher in action can be in imparting values. Judaism has always taught that exposure to a *tzaddik's* day-to-day behavior is a valued mode of absorbing practical lessons about how to lead a proper life.

There is a major difference between moral knowledge and moral action — *knowing* what is right and *acting* on this knowledge. A child can *know* exactly what is expected of him in a given situation, yet not *act* on this knowledge when actually faced with a moral dilemma. The Chofetz Chaim told the following story to illustrate this concept: There was a landowner who had to leave town for an extended period of time. Before embarking on his trip he left the responsibility for supervising his properties to his trusted overseer who was given a detailed "to do" list that described a series of tasks that were to be done during the landowner's absence. Upon the latter's return everything was in a state of chaos. The landowner severely chastised the overseer for neglecting his duties, reminding him that he had left him a detailed list of his duties. The overseer defensively protested, "But I read the list every morning!" The Chofetz Chaim explained that the same is true of Jews who are meticulous in their study of Torah, but not as careful in putting their Torah knowledge into practice. Teaching our children the *Shulchan Aruch* (The Code of Law), without providing active guidance regarding the actual implementation of this knowledge in the real world, is analogous to the overseer reading and not implementing his *to do* list.

Robert Coles, a Harvard child-psychiatrist, who is a leading expert on instilling values in children, relates a very powerful story in his book on this topic: A young woman who had taken several courses he taught on moral development came to his office to inform him that she was leaving Harvard. Dr. Coles was surprised to hear this, since the woman came from a small town that took great pride in sending one of its own to such a prestigious college. She explained that she had to put herself through college by cleaning rooms in the university's dormitories. One of those rooms was occupied by the student who consistently received the highest grade in Dr. Cole's classes on morality, a young man who came from a wealthy home. She bitterly related to Dr. Coles how, when she came to clean this student's room, he did everything he could to demean her and taunt her for being a cleaning lady. She left Harvard, telling Dr. Coles that she could not be part of an institution that could reward such an immoral individual with top grades in the very area in which he was so deficient. As a university professor once said regarding a top student, "He always got an A in my course, but ultimately he got an F in life."

Mental health professionals and educators who work with "at-risk" children have noted the unexpected healing powers of giving alienated adolescents a chance to do *chessed*. I have repeatedly seen the transforming effects of giving such children a chance to find meaning by affording them an opportunity to achieve success and recognition by helping others.

> *A 17-year-old boy was becoming increasingly defiant of his parents and teachers. He stayed out practically all night, associating with friends who had dropped out of school and who were experimenting with drugs. He was on the verge of being expelled from his school because he slept late, missed most of his classes and completed none of his*

assignments. The boy's principal had a "hunch" that he could kill two birds with one stone. The principal assigned the youngster to work with a neurologically impaired special education student who attended the lower school. This student had frequent explosive tantrums and even the most experienced special education teachers were having difficulty controlling him. The rebellious adolescent was able to reach the young child in a manner that was unprecedented. He was patient with him and seemed to be able to get him to cooperate with his teachers in a way that short-circuited the boy's explosive outburst. He was ultimately given a job as a paid aide for this child and received so much praise and recognition for his role in turning the child around that he once again felt connected to his family and school. No longer feeling marginalized, he gave up his street friends and an arrangement was worked out for him to finish high school by taking courses that were built around his job.

The positive impact of requiring our children to perform acts of *chessed* is also evident with mainstream children. Several summers ago a fascinating event took place in a large summer camp. As an experiment, this camp added some bunks populated with children who had special needs. These children, who were diagnosed with mental retardation, mild autism and various other developmental disabilities, took part in the camp's activities together with the other children. A totally unintended outcome emerged. It was expected that the children with special needs would benefit from being included in activities with the mainstream. What was totally unexpected, however, was the way this experience transformed the manner in which the mainstream children interacted with one another. After several weeks, the children and staff noticed that the whole atmosphere of the camp had changed. Children started to be kinder to each other. The cliques and competitiveness that often characterize interaction between children had vanished. It seems that once these children had been required to go beyond themselves and perform *chessed* with children less fortunate than themselves, their acts of kindness became contagious, and they were more kind and tolerant in *all* their interactions.

The most obvious subtle transmitter of values occurs when we unconsciously model proper behavior for our children. Every time a husband and wife resolve a disagreement with calm, respectful discussion they are modeling how to deal with disagreements with others in a respectful way. Each time parents enter a museum or amusement park and tell the truth about their children's age, even though they could easily lie and get less expensive children's tickets, a powerful lesson about honesty is transmitted. In countless ways parental interaction with others conveys messages that shape impressionable children's sense of what is right and wrong. Transmitting values to children is a constant process that is formed by the climate of values that pervades our homes. When parents set a tone of honesty, guidance, kindness and genuine respect for others, children absorb these values and grow into adults who, in turn, take part in the intergenerational transmission of what it means to be a Jew.

◅ঽ Instilling Honesty/Integrity

The *Midrash* (*Midrash Rabbah, Parshah* 8) teaches us that when God was about to create man there was a difference of opinion among the angels. *Tzedek*, the attribute of Righteousness, and *Chessed,* the attribute of Kindness, argued in favor of the creation of man, since he is "inherently righteous and kind." The attributes of *Shalom*, Peace, and *Emes,* Truth, argued against man's creation, since man is "thoroughly contentious and thoroughly false." God responded by taking Truth and hurling it to the ground. Thus, God made room for the creation of man by temporarily setting aside Truth.

The Kotzker Rebbe asks an obvious question. Why did God choose to cast down Truth and not Peace? Didn't Peace also argue against man's creation? The Rebbe answers that when something is cast down to the ground it fragments. When God threw down Truth it broke into pieces and is thus, by definition, no longer Truth. It had been shattered, and since Truth brooks no compromise it was neutralized and was no longer a factor in deciding for or against the creation of man. On the other hand, if

God had thrown down Peace it too would have broken into pieces as well. However, as the Kotzker said, *"A shtikel shalom iz oych shalom"* — "A little Peace is also Peace." In contrast to Truth, Peace is not an all-or-nothing concept. Even a little bit of Peace between husband and wife, or parent and child, is better than no Peace at all. Alternatively, there is no compromise with Truth, it demands total integrity and completeness.

It is of note, that the ally of Truth in the *Midrash* was *"Shalom,"* a word that not only means Peace but is also related to the word *sheleimus* – completeness or integrity. The word *integrity* is defined in the dictionary as "the quality of being whole or undivided, completeness."[1] The root of the word is from the Latin word *integritas,* which is based on the word *integer* meaning *whole* or *complete.*

This concept is further reflected in the Hebrew word for Truth (*Emes*), which is spelled *aleph, mem, tuf* — the first, middle and last letters of the Hebrew alphabet. The very word *Emes* implies integrity — something that is whole and all-encompassing from the start, through the middle and until the very end. In contrast, the Hebrew word for falsehood (*Sheker*) is spelled with letters that are close to one another alphabetically, and out of order — *shin, kuf, reish.* The lesson is clear. The forces of *Sheker* find it easy to unite, while those of Truth find the quest for integrity and unity to be more elusive, requiring a longer haul (from *aleph* through *tuf*).

The *Maharal* in *Avos* (1:18) further highlights the lessons to be learned from the physical attributes of the letters spelling *Emes* and *Sheker.* The letters of *Emes* symbolize solidity and stability, as signified by the two *legs* that form the foundation of both the letter *aleph* and *tuf,* and the long base of the *mem.* In contrast, the expression "Falsehood has no feet" (*Tikunei Zohar* 425) is graphically portrayed by the three letters of *Sheker* that sit shakily on a point: *Shin,* in Torah script (unlike the printed form in today's books), comes to a point, as do *kuf* and *reish.* From the standpoint of parenting, the wisdom

---

[1] *American Heritage Dictionary of the English Language,* Fourth edition, Houghton Mifflin, 2000.

inherent in these two words carries a powerful lesson. To imbue our children with the sense of stability that honesty and integrity engender requires much diligence and effort. Conversely, in a society rampant with *Sheker*, the draw toward deceit and falsehood can easily pull our children toward an unstable and slippery slope.

The central role of Truth is described by King David in *Psalms* (85:12), *Truth grows from the earth.* The Kotzker Rebbe asks, "Since everything that grows needs a seed, what seed must be planted to yield a crop of *Emes*?" He answered. "If you bury falsehood, then truth will grow." The seed of *Emes* begins by uprooting and burying dishonesty. If we live in a society where *Sheker* is rampant, then Truth can only be cultivated by training ourselves and our children to recognize and reject an atmosphere of dishonesty that can be so pervasive that we are not even aware of it.

The pervasive pull of the forces of *Sheker* is well illustrated by a national survey of 12,000 high school students conducted in 2002 by the Josephson Institute of Ethics. The percentage of adolescents admitting they cheated on an exam at least once in the past year jumped by 13 percent compared to the previous decade (61 percent in 1992 vs. 74 percent in 2002.). Similar trends were found in the percentage of high school students who acknowledged lying to parents or teachers. In just two years (2000-2002), there was an 11 percent increase in the number of secondary school students who reported that they would be willing to lie to get a good job (28 percent to 39 percent).

The 2002 report also reported an alarming finding. Common sense would dictate that adolescents attending religious schools would demonstrate higher levels of honesty than public school students. The survey found that students who attend private religious schools relative to their public school counterparts were marginally more likely to cheat on exams (78 percent vs. 72 percent) than their public school counterparts. They were also somewhat more likely to lie to their teachers (86 percent vs. 81 percent).

In contrast to their behavior and attitudes, adolescents clearly *know* the difference between right and wrong. Their parents have communicated a message that has led to an intellectual message that their child should do the right thing regardless of negative consequences. In the survey, 84 percent agree with the statement, "My parents want me to do the ethically right thing, no matter what the cost." Similarly, 93 percent said that their parents would prefer that they get bad grades rather than cheat on tests. As in so many other areas of life there is a difference between moral knowledge and moral action. Knowing that honesty is the right approach is very different from acting honestly when having to face the unpleasantness of doing poorly on a test or assignment. Taking the easy way out by cheating appears to have reached epidemic proportions.

The increase in cheating is also evident in the college-age population. The Center for Academic Integrity at Duke University reports that approximately 70 percent of college students admit to cheating, and 95 percent of them claim that they have never been caught. Likewise, Donald McCabe of Rutgers University conducted a survey in 1999 of thousands of students on 21 campuses across the country. Approximately one-third admitted to serious test cheating and half acknowledged at least one episode of serious cheating on written assignments. When asked to explain how they rationalize their dishonesty, most of the students attributed their actions to what they view as the unrealistic pressures they face. For example, they say that they feel compelled to cheat because of the demands placed on them to excel academically for the purposes of getting into the "right" graduate school or job. These studies also document a pervasive attitude on the part of faculty at the secondary and university level that makes them reluctant to take action against suspected cheaters. In spite of the pervasiveness of cheating, less than half of 800 faculty surveyed on 16 campuses in 1992 say they have ever reported a student for cheating. In a 1999 survey of over 1,000 faculty members on 21 campuses, one-third of those who were aware of student cheating in their course in the last two years, did nothing to address it. It should come as no surprise that students report that academic dishonesty is higher in courses where it is well known that faculty members are likely to ignore their cheating.

Unfortunately, our community is not immune to this problem. As noted earlier, parents typically teach their children how to arrive at an intellectual awareness of the importance of acting truthfully and honestly. The parental role of teaching children not to cheat in school requires an increased awareness of the multiple ways that indirect messages, in this area, are transmitted to our children. For the segment of our community that places great value on having their children attend highly selective colleges, intense parental focus on grades and SAT scores at the expense of developing high levels of integrity and moral behavior transmits a powerful lesson as to what *really* matters. Of course, equally powerful lessons are transmitted to our children if they are exposed to parental dishonesty in business or paying taxes. Even more subtle but, perhaps, equally important messages are conveyed to children, for example, every time they are told to falsely tell a telemarketer or *meshulach* (collector for charity) that the parent is not home, when parents exaggerate about their achievements to a friend, or lie to a police officer to avoid getting a ticket. Such behavior can provide powerful, albeit unintended lessons regarding honesty.

In Tractate *Shabbos* (55a), Rav Chanina teaches us: "The signature of Hashem is Truth." Artists are often known by their signature piece — the song or piece of art that defines them. *L'havdil* (to distinguish), God's signature piece is *Emes*. The teachers of ethical values teach us that since man is created *"b'tzelem Elokim,"* in God's image, engaging in falsehood violates one's own *tzelem Elokim*. In essence, our Rabbis teach us that cheating, deceit and lying are akin to negating the part of us that is Godlike. Like a counterfeiter who forges another's signature, *Sheker* makes us guilty of forging Hashem's signature. The role of parents is to help their children understand that cheating goes beyond the obvious costs of dishonesty. By cheating they are impairing their human dignity, the essence of their connectedness to Hashem.

◄֮ Instilling Values Regarding Money

For more than four decades the American Council on Education, and UCLA have together surveyed nearly one quarter of a million entering college freshmen in the United States, asking them to rank their primary life goals. In 1965, 82 percent said that developing a meaningful philosophy of life was essential, while only 42 percent said that earning a good living was essential. In contrast, in 1998, only 35 percent endorsed the finding of meaning as a core goal, while 74 percent ranked being very welloff financially at the top of their list.

In what is termed by psychologists "The American Paradox," researchers have found that while (corrected for inflation) Americans are twice as rich, there has been no corresponding rise in levels of happiness and satisfaction with life. In fact, during the same period of time that real income has doubled in the United States there has been a doubling of the divorce rate and the rates of adolescent suicide have tripled. In what some mental health experts term "affluenza," the rate of depression in affluent adolescents has increased substantially. It appears that when children are taught to value money instead of more enduring sources of meaning, such as religion, family and friends, their risk for leading empty, unfulfilling lives increases significantly.

While an excessive emphasis on the importance of money risks a focus on superficial materialism, it is also important to teach children about the value of earning money through their own efforts rather than consistently feeling entitled to receive money from their parents for whatever they want or need. There are numerous ways that overindulgence can negatively impact on a child. Not only can possessions come to lose their value, but children are at risk of failing to learn the crucial benefits of self-discipline. A powerful indicator of this dynamic is the difference many educators observe in the lost and found sections of yeshivas in affluent communities as compared to those in communities that are financially less fortunate. Electronic games, toys and expensive coats worth hundreds of dollars often go unclaimed in the lost and founds of the wealthy schools, while very little of value goes unclaimed in the yeshivas in the less affluent neighborhoods. When possessions are so easily replaced that they have little value to children, we are in danger of producing spoiled and overindulged children.

Psychologists emphasize the crucial importance of teaching children how to learn the connection between effort and reward. When a child demands possessions with no corresponding requirement to earn it, he or she is deprived of learning self-discipline — a skill that is essential to leading a successful life. The Jewish attitude toward money clearly emphasizes the importance of understanding the value of earning money through one's own efforts rather than receiving it as a gift. The *Talmud Yerushalmi* (*Orlah* 1:3) speaks of *"nehama d'kesufa,"* "bread of shame," regarding the psychological discomfort that individuals feel when their basic needs are met without any effort on their part. The Talmud explains that one who eats the food of another is ashamed to look at his benefactor's face. A corollary of this psychological truth can be found in the words of Rav Kahana: "An individual prefers one portion of his own over nine belonging to his friend" (*Bava Metzia* 38a). Finally, in an insight that helps explain the high rate of depression in affluent adolescents who have everything handed to them on a silver platter, the Talmud teaches us: "The world looks dark to somebody who depends on the sustenance of others" (*Beitzah* 32b).

The *Midrash* teaches us that when the Third *Beis HaMikdash* (The Holy Temple) will be established it will come down from heaven fully built except for the gates and doors, which we will have to add ourselves. As the *Midrash* explains, the gates of the Temple were consumed and, at the time of the third Temple, will be excavated and put in place through our own efforts (*Bamidbar Rabbah, Parshah* 15). The obvious question is if God is ready to give us the Third *Beis HaMikdash,* why not give it to us complete? The valuable lesson learned from this is that it is important to always take an active role. Even at the time of redemption, when we are so fully in God's hands, we must do our share by taking an active role in reestablishing the Temple. Otherwise, our rejoicing in the redemption will have an element of overdependence — of *nehama d'kesufa.*

Recent research in psychology has consistently documented the benefits of requiring that children actively pitch in and help out with the tasks that busy families need in order to function efficiently. Several studies have found that in families going through chronic stresses, such as financial pressures or illness, it is protective to require that children go beyond themselves by pitching in and helping the family. Obligating children to help out with everyday chores and tasks can give such children a sense of control and fulfillment. Obviously, it is important that these children not be overburdened by being assigned an unreasonable load that can rob them of their childhood. Researchers suggest that the following ingredients are characteristic of appropriate required helpfulness:

- Age-appropriate responsibility that the child can handle.
- Responsibilities that do not interfere with the age-appropriate tasks of childhood.
- Responsibilities accompanied by clear and consistent expectations of what is required of the child.

While the Jewish and psychological perspectives on the importance of not indulging one's children are clear, many parents find it difficult not to be overindulgent. To counter these tendencies it is important to examine some of the internal and external forces that may serve to feed this potentially destructive force. Parents should engage in a *cheshbon hanefesh* (mental and spiritual self-examination) regarding why they have difficulty not giving their children everything they want. Some common reasons include trying to keep up with friends, a misguided attempt to be *fair* by giving children what their friends have, or discomfort with our children's tantrums when they are denied what they are asking for. Another increasing contributor to overindulgence occurs in families where both parents work and are often unable to spend enough time with their children. At times, in these families, parents give their children material possessions in an attempt to replace themselves. Another subtle, perhaps unconscious force feeding this tendency is found in parents, who might have grown up with very little, who give too much to their children as a means of vicariously enjoying that which they were themselves unable to enjoy in their own childhood.

Psychologists suggest that the first step in developing an approach that transmits healthy values about money to our children is increased awareness of our own attitudes toward money. Lee Hausner, a psychologist who specializes in this area, suggests that parents should ask themselves the following questions:

- What was the attitude of each of your parents toward money and how did this affect you?
- What did you learn about money from watching other family members and friends?
- What does money mean to you now? What do you see as its greatest value / its greatest danger?
- What attitudes about money would you like to teach your children? What changes would you like to make?[2]

Recommendations:

- Children should be reminded to thank parents for what they may take for granted — for help with homework, for a lift to a friend's house, or even for preparing dinner. Parents should resist any tendency to inadvertently sabotage this lesson by responding with phrases like, "Don't mention it." Instead, children should be praised for expressing gratitude. Acting as a role model by expressing gratitude to others, in front of your children, is another powerful lesson in instilling this core Jewish value.

- Monitor children's exposure to angry discussions about others. Parents often underestimate the degree to which children are tuned in to marital disputes or criticism of friends, family, or educators. If such discussions must take place, make sure that children are not eavesdropping.

- Deal with a child's disrespect calmly and firmly. Parents may have no immediate control over a child's inappropriate statements, but they do have ultimate control over consequences for such disrespect. Logical consequences that directly flow from the child's lack of respect are often the most effective. For example, a parent may respond to a child's *chutzpah* by refusing to do something that he or she normally does for that child, such as providing a lift to a friend's house. Consequences that

[2] Hausner, Lee (1990), *Children of Paradise: Successful Parenting for Prosperous Families,* Archer, Los Angeles.

are of a shorter duration tend to be more effective than drawn-out punishments or those that are not time-limited.
- Children should be actively encouraged to become involved in *Chessed* projects. Many opportunities abound, ranging from organizations like *Tomchei Shabbos*, to working with ill children, or those with special needs. Projects should be suited to children's interest and temperament and should **never** be forced on children.

◄᠊ᡖ Parental Interventions Regarding Cheating

If a child is found to be cheating at school, a frank, planned, unemotional discussion is called for. This is a perfect time to share your view about how seriously you value honesty. Arriving at an understanding of the underlying forces that led to your child's cheating is an essential component of preventing future incidents. Try to elicit your child's view as to how he justified the cheating to himself. Creating an atmosphere that allows for such a discussion will entail a combination of finding the balance between parental calmness while conveying how seriously you value honesty. To insure that your child does not become overly defensive, make clear that whatever consequence you will deliver for this serious infraction will be tempered by the child's willingness to honestly discuss how he or she can try to avoid the temptation to cheat in the future.

Examine how competition is handled in the family. How does your child handle competition on the playground, in playing board games with siblings or peers? These venues can provide valuable lessons that can teach healthy competition while avoiding internal pressure to cheat.

Examine your expectations — particularly how you handle situations where your child disappoints you with poor academic performance. You may need to work on yourself by adjusting your expectations regarding your child's ability to achieve. Let your child know that much as you value his or her performing well in school, you place a higher value on honesty in the face of pressure. You can say, "I understand the temptation to cheat, particularly when you feel that you are under a lot of pressure, but I'm disappointed when you aren't honest. Telling the truth is far more important to me than your grades."

If the underlying issue is your child's difficulty to keep up with unrealistic academic demands, work with your child's teacher and principal to modify the curriculum in a manner that creates more realistic academic goals. Parents are often pleasantly surprised by the willingness of the school to accommodate their academic demands to a child's specific needs.

As in other areas of parenting, logical consequences that make sense to your child work best. If the child was caught cheating, help him or do proper *teshuvah* (here, make reparation) by having him or her make up for the action. If he or she was caught copying a term paper, supervise the writing and resubmitting of an alternative assignment. If your child was caught cheating on a test, try to work as a team with the school in arriving at a logical punishment. It makes sense, however, to work with the teacher in arranging a retest after offering your child support in mastering the work being tested.

৵ৎ *Instilling Proper Values Regarding Money*

It can be helpful for parents to monitor the content of the conversations that their children are exposed to around the home. How much talking is there about goods and possessions? Is the focus of adult conversation often centered on new construction in the home, the need to buy a better car or computer? If this is the primary focus of parental discussion, then children are more likely to learn to value materialism over more meaningful values.

Help your children learn to distinguish between *wants* and *needs*. When planning to buy them gifts for birthdays or Chanukah, help them write wish lists that require that they prioritize what they want — making clear that they will not get everything that they ask for.

If your child has frequent tantrums when not given what he or she asks for, help him or her (after a calming-down period) to identify the underlying emotion feeding the tantrum. What are the underlying issues? If the child is bored and wants a new toy to combat the boredom, what are other ways of helping tolerate this frustration? If the issue is that friends have this toy, discuss the underlying feelings of social insecurity, etc.

Remember that is is fine to say "No," and fine for your child to be upset. Children learn very valuable, lifelong lessons by being required to deal with the frustration of not getting everything they need or want.

Giving children a weekly allowance can be a helpful tool for teaching a responsible approach toward money. Until approximately age 8, children may have difficulty understanding the concept of savings. Early elementary school-age children can be taught, however, how to prioritize purchases. In the spirit of helping children distinguish *wants* from *needs* they can be encouraged to choose what they want most from their wish list. From third grade on, most children have a good understanding of the relationship between how much things cost and parents' ability to afford them. As children get older they can be given enough money on an incremental basis to gradually increase their responsibility for their purchases.

PART TWO

THE LEFT HAND PUSHING AWAY:

THE USE OF LIMIT-SETTING
IN BALANCED PARENTING

Chapter Five:
Setting Limits

O ne of the mechanisms which children and adolescents use to forge their sense of identity and independence is the testing of limits. Parents are often uncomfortable dealing with the anger and disappointment that they may engender when they say "No." Yet, this process is a healthy component of raising children with the right values. Parents who are unable to consistently and firmly set limits risk raising children who are defiant and have difficulty developing a finely tuned sense of inner control. As a wise man once said, "*No* is a giant's word" — i.e. it takes a big person to say "*No.*"

A recent national survey[1] found that two-thirds of parents in the United States believe that they spoil their children. The survey reported that 80 percent of 1,015 adults interviewed believed that children today are more spoiled than children 10 or 15 years ago. Three-fourths of those polled also said that they believe that children today have fewer chores than children in the past. In keeping with these findings, the most common questions I am asked when I give parenting lectures reflect a reluctance on the part of parents of this generation to place limits on their children. There seems to be a deeply ingrained belief, perhaps as result of the emphasis on validating and supporting children's

---

[1] Time-CNN poll, July 2001.

emotions at all costs, that if a child is upset by a restriction, the parents should back down or, at least, reconsider their position in light of the child's protests.

Psychologists have repeatedly found that children thrive in a family atmosphere that is authoritative — with parents who provide clear and firm direction in a context of warmth and open communication.[2] Research has documented that families that take an overly laissez-faire approach with their children increase the risks of poor self-esteem, depression and drug use.[3]

We are taught, *Discipline your child, because there is hope; let your soul not be swayed by his protest (Proverbs 19:18).* A *midrash* on this verse tells us the opposite of what one would expect: *The more one disciplines one's child the more the child will love his parent (Shemos Rabbah1).* When loving parents are faced with an upset and crying child, it is only natural to have second thoughts and be tempted to give in to the child's demands. Keep in mind, however, that beneath his or her protests there is often a part of the child that welcomes the structure and limits.

A number of years ago I counseled an adolescent who had problems of serious conflict with his parents. His home was dominated by frequent arguments with his parents who, he felt, were placing stricter limits on him than those placed by the parents of any of his peers. Currently, as he is a young parent himself, he recently told me that when he thinks back to his years of resisting his parents' rules, he is very grateful that they never yielded to his protests. He now realizes that their limit-setting was necessary and was derived from their understanding that they had to fulfill their responsibility to protect him from himself. What he had previously viewed as arbitrary and cruel, he now saw as loving and responsible. What I found of particular interest, however, was his assertion that he remembers, even during the worst periods of conflict,

---

[2] Baumrind, D. (1968), "Authoritarian vs. an authoritative control," *Adolescence,* 3:255-272.

[3] Furnham, A. & Cheng, H. (2000), "Perceived parental behavior, self-esteem and happiness," *Social Psychiatry, Psychiatric Epidemiology,* 35:463-470.

that he was secretly happy that his parents stood firm. He was frightened at the time about the temptations to which he was being exposed and, although he could barely acknowledge it to himself, let alone his parents, he needed the controls that he was unable to provide for himself.

A research study conducted approximately 15 years ago by a well-known psychologist investigated the various forms adolescent rebellion might take in different parts of the world. In an interview with a group of teens in Amish country, where there are strict rules against engaging in any kind of contemporary behavior, the researcher asked what constitutes getting into trouble in their neighborhood. The Amish teens sheepishly answered that sometimes, when their more defiant peers are in the mood for mischief, they wear a pink handkerchief in their jacket pocket. When asked to describe the worst case of misbehavior in memory, they told the story of a teen in a neighboring town who was once caught hitching a ride on a tractor. As part of the same study, a group of adolescents in Lebanon, at the height of their civil war, said that the only way to truly rebel was to open fire on members of their own clan. One of the more important lessons learned from this study is that children and adolescents often define themselves by testing the upper limits placed on them by their parents. Wherever the line is drawn, and as part of the normal process of internalizing their parents' values, youngsters need to test parental resolve to enforce rules. In Amish society, the line is drawn at a very different place than in Lebanon, but if a limit is not placed, or not enforced, the chances increase that children will stray into dangerous areas.

A teenage boy attending a yeshivah high school was referred for counseling because of increasingly rebellious behavior. He came from a home where there was a great deal of love and attention but very little in the way of setting limits. Mildly rebellious behavior gradually gave way to an out-of-control situation in which he was staying out all night, and experimenting with drugs. In a family therapy meeting with this youngster and his parents, they firmly told him that the rules of the house were changing, and they set down a new set of rules including a strict curfew and careful guidelines about his chores, academic responsibilities and the consequences of noncompliance. The young man became increasingly angry as his parents were reviewing these changes. As his tantrum escalated I feared that if I didn't contain the situation, there was danger of physical violence. I asked the parents to leave the room, and after several minutes of silence, the boy calmed down, let out a sigh, and said, "It's about time!" This served as a turning point for the family, and the rebellious behavior gradually gave way to significant improvement.

◄⅞ Jewish Perspectives on Setting Limits

The Talmud teaches that the key to raising successful children is to find the balance between *the left hand that pushes away, and the right hand that draws closer (Sanhedrin* 107b). This balance between limit-setting and emotional connection is totally consistent with current psychological thinking. Child-psychologists tell us that rules without relationships often result in rebellion. When children know that their parents' limit-setting takes place in the context of love and caring, they are far less likely to seriously challenge parental rules. A beautiful insight into this Talmudic passage was shared by Rabbi Simcha Wasserman, who asked what would happen if one would *literally* carry out the advice of the Talmud by simultaneously pushing a child with one's left hand while drawing him closer with the right hand. The result, said Rabbi Wasserman, is that the child will be turned around. In fact, if one wishes to distill the essence of the art of child-rearing, it is the turning around of children by finding the correct balance between love and limits.

The *Midrash* teaches us that Phineas never died; in fact, he and Elijah were the same person (*Bamidbar Rabbah* 21:3). There is an interesting duality in the Torah's description of Phineas and Elijah — both of whom represent qualities essential for successful parenting. Phineas initially gained prominence as a zealot who defended Hashem's honor by killing those who sinned brazenly.

He knew when a situation called for a high level of firmness, fire and passion. But he was also known for his ability to bring peace. When there was concern that the tribes of Reuven and Gad were separating themselves from the mainstream of Jewish life, it was Phineas who was chosen to be the emissary to make peace.

It is noteworthy that of all the personalities in the Bible, Elijah is the one chosen as the paradigm for peaceful relationship between fathers and sons, *And he will turn back [to God] the hearts of fathers with [their] sons and the hearts of sons with their fathers* (*Malachi* 3:24). Elijah is the perfect messenger for peace between the generations because of his ability to integrate the two components necessary for effective parenting — love and limits — *the left hand pushes away, while the right hand draws closer.* When Elisha was appointed to take Elijah's place he requests, *May twice as much of your spirit be mine* (*II Kings* 2:9). Isn't it unseemly and presumptuous for a disciple to make such a request of his teacher and mentor? What in fact Elisha was asking Elijah was to teach him the secret of integrating the passion of zealotry with the measured tolerance that his *rebbi* demonstrated in his role as peacemaker. As Elisha assumes the mantle of leadership he requests that he too be given the ability to integrate the the dual components of Elijah's character — the ability to draw on the fire and passion necessary to be an effective leader and teacher, coupled with the ability to bring peace. Both elements, though seemingly paradoxical, are essential ingredients necessary for *turning back the hearts of fathers with [their] sons.*

In the weekly portion *Bo,* the Torah refers to the *"tam"* — the simple son — who relates to the story of the history of our freedom by merely asking, "What is this?" (*Exodus* 13:14). He has so little knowledge and education that he is only able to ask the simplest of questions. What happened to his education? Why didn't his parents equip him with the ability to relate to our history in a more mature manner? The answer to this unspoken question is in the verse, *And it shall be a sign upon your arm* (*Exodus* 13:16). The unusual spelling of the Hebrew word for *your arm* with the seemingly superfluous letter *hei* at the end is explained by our rabbis as meaning, *a weak hand*. Although we learn a *halachic* principle from this unusual spelling, namely that *tefillin* should be placed on the weaker arm, there is also a great moral lesson that is implied by this odd spelling. The Torah is subtly teaching us why the simple son is so deficient in his knowledge. It is because his parents did not exercise their authority over him in his formative years. Their hand was weak. Homiletically, the meaning of *And it shall be a sign* is that this child is an indicator of his parents' *weak hand*. Education and growth can thrive only when parents are willing to impose the firm structure and limits necessary for raising an informed Jew.

The *Midrash* (*Bereishis Rabbah* 97) relates an incident that contains an important lesson on the topic of setting limits with children. When Jacob's children prepared to bury him in the Cave of Machpelah, Esau tried to restrain them, demanding proof of title. When Chushim, the deaf son of Dan, saw Esau interfering with the burial of his grandfather, he immediately killed his great-uncle. Rabbi Chaim Shmulevitz asks an obvious question: Why didn't Jacob's children object to the delay caused by Esau? Wasn't it out of character for the brothers, who were typically such action-oriented individuals, to fail to defend their father's honor? What about our duty to insure that we honor the deceased? Rabbi Shmulevitz answers that as a deaf man Chushim was not drawn into Esau's irrelevant arguments. There are times that *seeing* an insulting act rather than *hearing* about it illuminates and clarifies a situation. Robbed of the power of hearing, Chushim was able to cut to the heart of the matter and perceive the situation with greater clarity. The lesson for parents is an important one. Certain circumstances call for action rather than negotiation.

A story illustrating this point is told about a generous-spirited man who was hounded by numerous acquaintances who constantly requested favors. One man, in particular, repeatedly took advantage of his kindness. Upon receiving a letter, yet again, asking for money, the benefactor wrote back, "In response to your request for another loan, my answer is 'No,' and in order that you know that my answer is final, I give you no reason." There are times in parenting that call for a calm and reasoned explanation for refusing to grant a child's request, but there are also times, particularly when a child presents endless arguments and perseveres with persistent whining, when the appropriate answer is "No" — without an explanation.

Although sometimes parents must deal with their children by firmly saying "No," there are also occasions when parenting calls for flexibility. The Talmud in *Taanis* (20a) teaches us: *A man should always be pliable as a reed, rather than unyielding as a cedar.* Even though, at a superficial level, a cedar tree appears stronger than a reed, in fact, a reed's fragility is deceptive. During a storm a reed bends without breaking, while a cedar tree is more likely to be destroyed. Part of the art of parenting is knowing when to bend and show flexibility and when to stand firm. As this Talmud passage teaches us, although this might appear as a weakness, it is, in fact, a sign of strength.

A related issue with regard to limit-setting is the tendency of children to drag parents into fruitless power struggles while trying to get children to comply. Rabbi Dessler, in *Michtav M'Elijah*, has likened this process to that of pushing one's hand against a mattress. The more pressure one exerts, the more resistance one experiences from the spring of the mattress. The struggle stops as soon as one ceases pushing. In effectively enforcing rules, it is important to recognize that when parents find themselves locked in such battles the short-term solution is often to temporarily disengage. A child will often lessen his resistance when his parents stop pushing.

The Talmud in *Yevamos* (121a) relates an incident in which Rabbi Akiva survived a shipwreck. When Rabbi Gamliel, who witnessed the event, asked Rabbi Akiva how he survived, Rabbi Akiva answered, *"The plank of a ship came my way, I grabbed hold to stay afloat, and I bent my head to every wave that approached."* The lesson learned from this, says the Talmud, is that if a man is confronted with a force that threatens to engulf him, *let him bend his head* and not fight it.

A similar approach is implied in the lives of three giants of Jewish history. The *Midrash Tanchuma* (*Vayechi* 6) teaches us that three great men responded to conflict by strategically retreating: *David fled from King Saul and his son Absalom, Moses (from Pharaoh) and Jacob from his brother, Esau ... They temporarily conceded to the demands of the moment.*

This teaches us that it is better to *bow your head* than resist when threatened by a situation where there is little hope that a head-on approach will be immediately effective. As a related *midrash* concludes, *Whoever resists being sucked in by the demands of the moment succumbs, whoever bides their time ultimately prevails* (*Yalkut Shimoni, Exodus* 2:168).

In applying the principle of *biding one's time* to parenting, it is important to keep in mind that such an approach is not considered *giving in*. On the contrary, Jacob, Moses and David ultimately prevailed. Their victory was a matter of having the patience and wisdom to know when to temporarily withdraw and when to actively engage.

In summary, the art of raising children is having the wisdom to know which situations call for firm limit-setting without lengthy negotiations, which call for active discussion and negotiation and which call for ignoring or even for indulgence. Rabbi Yisroel Salanter used the following story to illustrate the need for such an approach in achieving this type of balance: A man, holding a bird in his hand, enters into a wager with another man as to whether the bird he is holding is alive or dead. He calculates that this is a sure bet: If the other man says the bird is alive, he will squeeze the bird to death; if the bet is that the bird is dead, he will open his hand and let the bird fly away. The other person, realizing this strategy, wisely answers, "It's in your hands." In finding the balance in disciplining children, it is indeed in the parents' hands — do not smother them by squeezing too tight while, at the same time, do not lose them by completely letting go.

Recommendations regarding limit-setting

■ Choosing which limits to place on children is a constantly evolving process informed by each child's age and temperament. Since consistency in enforcing limits is crucial, parents should carefully choose which rules are worthy battlegrounds. When parents place too many rules or limits on children they can compromise the happy atmosphere of the house and find themselves constantly disciplining.

- As noted earlier, rules without relationships result in rebellion. The key to effective limit-setting is the quality of the parent-child relationship. Limits are far easier to enforce in the context of a warm and loving relationship.
- Periodic calm conversations with your children regarding the rules of the home can be particularly helpful. Children are far more likely to comply when they understand the reasoning behind the family's rules.
- Nagging children via repetitive reminders may prove futile. Children often develop "parent deafness" when nagged. Similarly, lecturing a child by sharing insights or lessons from your own life almost never works. Children rarely respond to such talks by saying, "I hadn't thought of that, I'll change my ways." In the case of adolescents, in particular, one of the poignant realities of life is that parents can't save children from making the same mistakes that the parents may have made as teenagers. Children often have to find their own way. Before entering into such a discussion ask yourself how many times you have said the same thing before, and cue in to your adolescent's willingness to talk.
- Children do not have to like the limits placed by the parent; they only have to comply. Parents often fall into the trap of feeling that they have to engage in endless discussions with their child reexplaining why they are not allowing them to do something. This, too, is a by-product of the culture's emphasis on validating a child's feelings at all costs. If you are faced with a persistent, whining child who does not take "No" for an answer, you can use the following helpful techniques. Tell the child, "You may ask for that three more times." After the third request, ignore the protests. Thus, if your child is refusing to take "No" for an answer, calmly explain the reasoning behind denial of his request. The first

time he repeats his demand say, "That's once," without getting pulled into the content of the issue. The second time say, "That's twice," the third time, with as little anger as possible, answer, "That's the third time. Now I will ignore you." The advantage of this approach is that in a non-emotional way the parent is short-circuiting the process that typically ensues when the child "lawyers" the parents, engaging them in endless, fruitless discussions.

Chapter Six:
Controlling Anger in Dealing With Your Children

A consistent finding in research on parent-child relationships is that parents who frequently lose their temper with their children heighten the risk of behavioral and emotional difficulties in their children. As with adults, children respond best to calm and rational feedback. It is rare for adults to respond to angry criticism from a family member or from a colleague at work by calmly listening and accepting what is said. Children are even less likely than adults to integrate angry parental attempts to teach them, particularly when they are overwhelmed by the emotional impact of being on the receiving end of yelling or angry criticism.

A harsh disciplinary style that relies heavily on criticism, screaming, or physical punishment often appears to work with young children. However, the short-term effectiveness of an anger-based, punitive approach is very misleading. Numerous studies have shown that children raised in such an atmosphere learn to behave well when in front of their parents, but are far more likely to misbehave when they are away from them. Think back to your own days in school when the teacher who yelled and punished the most often had the most out-of-control class. Conversely, teachers with the best behaved classes are typically those who yell the least and praise the most. It should come as no surprise, therefore, that coercive styles of parenting are also associated with more resistance and problems from children.

Parenting experts recognize that parents who lose their temper when disciplining their children do so primarily because of a desire to teach proper values. Paradoxically, however, a child internalizes very little when anger dominates parental attempts to instill those values. The paradigm for the internalization of parental values is Joseph, who, when tempted by the wife of Potiphar, saw a likeness of his father, Jacob, flash in his consciousness at the very moment that he might have been tempted to betray his father's values (cf. *Sotah* 36b, quoted in *Rashi, Genesis* 39:11). This process of internalization is not drummed into a child's head by harsh parenting. On the contrary, Joseph, who was so beloved by his father, was far better able to carry within himself an internal representation of what was *right* because he had not been treated harshly when he deviated from the path set by his father.

In the long run, harsh parenting often comes back to haunt parents in the form of later rebelliousness. Rabbi Wolbe, in his book *Netiah U'Zeriah B'Chinuch,* notes that while parents can use physical punishment to force young children to bend to their will, they run a great risk of paying the price later, when, as adolescents or young adults, children can "vote with their feet" by leaving the way of life that was forced on them earlier.

This approach to child-rearing is codified in *Yoreh Dei'ah* (240:19): *It is forbidden to weigh down one's children with a heavy burden by being overly exacting with them, since this may prove to be a stumbling block. Instead, one should forgive them and ignore their lapses, because a father has the option of waiving the respect that is due him.*

It is noteworthy that the word *michshol* — stumbling block — used by the *Shulchan Aruch* parallels the prohibition in the Torah against placing an obstacle in front of the blind. The verse, *You shall not place a stumbling block before the blind* (*Leviticus* 19:14), is interpreted by our Sages as the prohibition against misleading a person. Parents, as guardians of the home, can mislead their children in a profound manner that goes beyond the immediate negative consequences of losing their temper with their children. The *Shulchan Aruch* is alluding to a longer-lasting consequence that emerges from engaging in an emotion-based rather than intellectually based style of discipline.

Clinical psychologists who design anger-management programs have found that the essence of successful anger control is the ability to pull back from the anger-provoking situation long enough to be able to think things through clearly. With the exception of safety issues, which, of course, require an immediate response, there are few situations that children can present to parents in which one cannot benefit from "striking when the iron is *cold*" — waiting until one's anger subsides. Rabbi Boruch Ber Leibowitz, who lived in pre-war Poland, would allow himself to vent his anger at his children only when he wore his special "anger hat." If he became angry, he would first go to find this special hat, put it on and only then allow himself to express his anger. Of course, by that time he had calmed down enough to deal with the situation in a more rational and productive manner.

An added advantage to controlling anger with children is that calm discussion sometimes reveals that the anger is not justified.

> *A rebbi of a third-grade class heard a lecture I gave about the importance of controlling one's temper in dealing with one's students. The lecture included the story mentioned earlier, of Rabbi Boruch Ber Leibowitz and his "anger hat." When I met the rebbi later that day, he told me that he was a little late for class that morning because of his attending the lecture. When he entered his classroom, one of his students looked at his watch as if to criticize the rebbi for being late. The rebbi's first reaction was to be furious. How dare a third grader give mussar to his rebbi! With the story of Rav Boruch Ber fresh in his mind, however, the rebbe figuratively waited to put on his "anger hat," and decided to wait until recess to deal with the child. As soon as recess began the boy came running excitedly to the rebbi, shouting "Rebbi! Rebbi! Look at the new watch I got for my birthday!"*

Stepping back from the anger-provoking situation allows the parent time to examine the rationality of his or her anger. The thoughts that accompany a tense interaction with one's child frequently trigger nonproductive and explosive parent-child confrontations. In my work with parents, I find that a powerful force that often underlies this anger is the mistaken belief that good parents must control their child's behavior at *all* times. Parents often tell me that the thoughts that cross their minds just before they lose their temper with their children are, "What's wrong with me that I have a child who acts this way?" or, "What's wrong with my child?" Such thoughts feed a sense of powerlessness and frustration — two feelings that inevitably lead to anger and an ineffective response.

Research on child development has documented that the more parents feel that they are not in control, the more likely they are to get caught up in angry and fruitless power struggles with their children. Feelings of helplessness in dealing with children are also associated, according to the research, with a tendency to ignore positive child behavior, as well as a predisposition to misread neutral behavior as malicious. The alternative is to react to a child's misbehavior in a manner that places a greater focus on what is, in fact, in your power. Instead of banging your head against the wall in a futile effort to make your child think, feel, or react as you want him to, recognize that at the time that your child is being particularly defiant, you may not have immediate control over his thoughts, feelings, or behavior. What you *do* have control over, however, is the ability to be firm, consistent and clear about what behavior you will tolerate, and the consequences for misbehavior. When faced with a defiant or noncompliant child, a parent should try to control the nonproductive thoughts that feed a feeling of powerlessness and replace them with a calm focus on an unemotional delivery of consequences for the misbehavior. In other words, be firm but not angry; be consistent while maintaining control of your actions, voice and emotions.

Another common pitfall is the anger-engendering belief that not only must children comply with parental requests, but that they should also be happy about doing what is asked of them. Although proper *derech eretz* should be expected of all children, in many cases their level of emotionalism and defiance can be reduced by insisting that they comply, while at the same time allowing them to respectfully express frustration. As long as a child is complying, long discussions aimed at robbing the child of his or her right to be upset are counterproductive. Parents do not have to rush to *do something* about a child's upset feelings.

⋙ Jewish Perspective on Anger

The *sifrei Mussar* (books on ethical values) teach us that, while anger has the potential to be one of the most destructive emotions, it can also serve an important purpose when controlled by the intellect rather than the heart.

King Solomon teaches us, *Rather, banish anger from your heart and remove evil from your flesh; for childhood and youth are futile (Ecclesiastes 11:10).* Angry, emotional outbursts are the mark of immaturity and childishness. Once we allow ourselves to be emotionally pulled into what psychologists call "the fool's circle" of our children's provocations, the anger is in control of us rather than the other way around.

The Talmud in *Pesachim* (66b) tells us that even a man as great as Moses lost his knowledge when he gave in to his anger. *Reish Lakish said: "Concerning any person who becomes angry, if he is a wise man, his wisdom departs from him; [we learn this] from Moses, for it is written: And Moses became angry at the commanders of the army ... (Numbers 31:14). And it is written: [And Elazar the Priest said to the men of the army who came to the war,] This is the decree of the Torah that Hashem commanded Moses (Numbers 31:21). This implies that the law was hidden from Moses [he forgot it]."*

As *Rashi* explains, Elazar taught the laws of koshering utensils instead of Moses, *because Moses came into the category of anger, he came into the category of error, for the laws of purging of [vessels that had been used for cooking by] non-Jews were concealed from him (Rashi, Numbers 31:21).* Moses' angry rebuke of his officers led him to forget the laws for koshering utensils. The individual who was the ultimate Torah authority and who was taught the Torah by the Almighty Himself lost his knowledge when he lost his temper — how much more so must we learn to control our anger.

At the beginning of *Ethics of the Fathers* we are taught about the central importance of the concept, *be deliberate in judgment* (*Ethics of the Fathers* 1:1) — we must be careful and circumspect when judging others. Calmness is also a central component in dealing wisely with children. It is impossible to properly judge and discipline a child in the midst of anger. If as great a man as Moses forgot what he knew because of his anger, imagine how greatly parental thinking and judgment is clouded by anger.

Maimonides summarizes the Jewish perspective on anger, conceit and pride as follows:

There are traits regarding which it is prohibited to strike a middle path. Rather, one should avoid these traits to the extreme. One of these traits is haughtiness. It is not enough to be humble — rather, one should be extremely humble. That is why it is written regarding Moses our teacher, "He was extremely humble," not just "humble." Therefore, our Rabbis taught us "be extremely humble," and they also taught us that anybody who is conceited is denying an essential aspect of our faith.

This is also the case with anger, which is a terrible trait. A person should avoid this trait to the extreme and teach himself not to become angry — even for a worthy reason. If he wants to instill fear in his children and household members, he should feign anger, but internally be calm (Hilchos Dei'os 2:3).

Maimonides categorizes anger as an emotion that needs to be completely uprooted from an individual's emotional repertoire. A parent who is disciplining a child should be calm and only feign anger. In such situations, the child is far more likely to recognize that the parent is acting for the child's own benefit and not because of an anger that comes from a feeling that one's authority is being challenged.

It is noteworthy that the only two personality traits that Maimonides teaches should be totally eradicated are *anger* and *pride*. From a psychological standpoint these two emotions are inextricably intertwined. Pride is ultimately at the root of many situations contributing to loss of one's temper. A frequent trigger of an angry parental response to a child's provocation is a thought process reflecting a feeling of "How does my child dare to do this to **me** after all I have done for him?" While such a reaction may be understandable, ideally we should strive to respond to our children from a calm perspective, motivated solely by our obligation to educate our children. In disciplining children, calm guidance and education should always supersede an anger fueled by injured pride.

A similar emphasis on the need to put anger completely under the control of the intellect is seen in the Kotzker Rebbe's explanation of the Mishnah in *Ethics of the Fathers, a protective fence for wisdom is silence* (*Ethics of the Fathers* 3:17). If silence is only the fence built around wisdom, what then is wisdom itself? The Kotzker Rebbe answers that even though one has taught him or herself to exercise self-control and not respond reflexively and angrily to an insult, still he or she is hurt and upset. He or she is silent, but is seething inside. The silence is merely a fence, which prevents him or her from reacting angrily to a provocation. True wisdom, however, is when a person is not even bothered by the insult, because he or she has learned how to be immune to the provocation of others. Hence, the slight has no impact on his or her emotions. Although this is an extremely difficult level to attain, it should serve as the ideal toward which we should all strive. The ultimate goal in parenting children calmly is the ability to guide and discipline them by filtering their provocative behavior through an intellectual rather than an emotional prism.

◄❧ The Interactive Nature of Anger

Angry interactions are often self-perpetuating. When parents have problems letting go of their anger with children who misbehave, the children typically respond in kind – with their own anger and continued misbehavior. This can engender and maintain a vicious cycle that does not allow for either parents or children to repair the situation. In a classic study, mothers referred for counseling because they were locked in repetitive, angry interaction with their rebellious children were asked to engage in videotaped unstructured play with them. The mothers were then asked to view the video and press a buzzer every time they were upset by something their child did during their play session. Relative to a group of comparison mothers, who did not have difficulties with their children, these mothers pressed the buzzer frequently, even when there was no clear provocation from their child. The reasoning behind this baffling perception was exemplified by one mother of a problem child who was asked why she pressed the buzzer to signal annoyance when her son requested a glass of orange juice during the play session. The mother angrily answered that six months earlier the child had spilled a glass of orange juice on a new carpet in their home. Her inability to let go of this anger continued to affect her interactions with her son, even a half a year after the incident!

The reciprocal nature of angry family interactions is portrayed in *Genesis* when Rebecca warns Jacob to run away from the danger of angry retaliation by his brother, Esau: *So now, my son, heed my voice and arise; flee to my brother Laban, to Charan. And remain with him a short while until your brother's wrath subsides. Until your brother's anger against you subsides and he forgets what you have done to him"* (Genesis 27:43-45).

The simple meaning of the phrase *until your brother's anger against you subsides* appears to be repetitious, since the previous verse already states, *until your brother's wrath subsides*. Additionally, given that the brothers are not living anywhere near each other and have no opportunities for interaction, how will Jacob know when his brother's wrath has subsided sufficiently for him to return home safely?

The son of Rabbi Chaim Volozhiner, Reb Itzel, explains that the words *until your brother's anger against you subsides* refer to Jacob, not Esau. Hence, these words are not repetitious. It is to be understood as Rebecca's response to the unarticulated question of Jacob as to how he will know that it is safe for him to return home. He will know, Rebecca implies, by examining his *own* emotional state and attitude toward Esau. When he feels that his anger toward his brother is diminished, then that will be a sign that Esau's anger toward him has also cooled. King Solomon expresses this thought in *Proverbs* when he states, *As water reflects a face back to a face, so one's heart is reflected back to him by another* (*Proverbs* 27:19).

How do I know how somebody feels about me? Often, the feeling toward me is a reflection of my feelings toward him or her. A parent's feelings toward a child are often complex and ambivalent. Even in the most tension-filled relationships, anger and tension are often mixed with love and admiration. Children know when their parents' continued anger and disappointment is reflected in subtle, often nonverbal interactions. If parents can find a way to reflect back their positive, loving feelings, rather than their anger, then negative interactions will likely give way to reflected feelings of reconciliation and love. The child will then respond in kind.

This important lesson was taught by Rebecca to Jacob, and is one that parents should apply to their interactions with their own children. Parents will often find that if they let go of their anger, children will respond in kind. As adults, it is our responsibility to take the first step, thereby providing a model of how to deal with anger responsibly — from the head, rather than from the heart.

In the case of parents who are dealing with alienated adolescents, their anger toward parents is, at times, so deep-seated that they will repel parental efforts at reconciliation. The lesson Rebecca taught Jacob is that in such situations parents should carefully examine their feelings toward their adolescent. If a point has been reached when a parent feels ready to resume calm interactions, without harboring lingering feelings of anger and resentment, it is likely that the adolescent, too, is ripe for reconciliation.

Recommendations:

■ Perhaps the greatest key to anger control is for parents to buy themselves time by not responding immediately. Parents need to recognize that delaying their responses to children's misbe-havior does not undermine parental effectiveness or authority.

■ Once the parent steps back and calms down, he or she should try to understand the situation from the child's perspective. The ability to see things through the prism of a child's eyes can have a tremendously calming effect on an angry parent. I recently saw a youngster who had been atypically irritable and defiant with his mother. After having a calm discussion with him, in which she tried to achieve an understanding as to why he had been so difficult in the weeks leading up to the discussion, she discovered that a classmate at school was teasing him merci-lessly. Her anger dissipated once she understood the source of her sons's irritability and, once she took action to help change the situation, his behavior and mood improved.

■ Another key component in anger control is learning to recog-nize the patterns and triggers of anger-provoking situations. Parents should systematically track what types of situations are likely to trigger angry interactions with their children. Once these patterns are understood, parents can either try to modify the situation before anger erupts, or remind themselves to step back from the situation early enough in the sequence to avoid an explosion.

■ Parental anger is inextricably intertwined with a child's angry response. An additional advantage to waiting until parental anger subsides before confronting the child is that the child is afforded an opportunity to calm down.

■ Parents should try to avoid spontaneous discussion about problems when their child is not motivated to talk. Make an appointment with your child to discuss issues of concern. State briefly and calmly what you want to discuss, agree on a time to get together and share your concerns after hearing your child's point of view.

Chapter Seven:
External Influences

An analogy that has been suggested to explain the impact of modern media on children is that of the "frog in the beaker." A frog that is thrown into a beaker of boiling water will try to save its life by jumping out of the beaker. If the same frog is thrown into a beaker containing water that is room temperature, on an oven range with a low simmering fire, he will boil to death. The temperature changes so gradually that the frog is not aware that it is in mortal danger. The changes to which children are exposed have been so gradual that we do not realize that the temperature is rapidly reaching a boiling point. In a very telling survey conducted by the Kaiser Foundation in February 2001,[1] a substantial increase in the sexual content of television situation comedies was found when compared to their previous survey, which had been conducted only two years previously. In that brief time span there was a 28 percent increase in the percentage of television situation comedies that contained sexual content (84 percent as compared to 56 percent only two years earlier). Perhaps most tellingly, 95 percent of these shows did not make even a passing reference to the risks and responsibilities of sexual activity. This represents a sea change in the temperature of the *water* in which our children

---

[1] "Sex on TV: A Biennial Report to the Kaiser Family Foundation" (2001), Washington, DC: The Henry J. Kaiser Family Foundation.

are immersed. Many parents who allow their children to watch these shows are not aware of how radically different they are from the shows they themselves may have watched as children.

The connection between television and aggression in children has also been studied extensively. The National Television Violence Study comprehensively examined aggressive content on television in the late 1990's.[2] They concluded that the average child witnesses 10,000 acts of violence a year, with over 60 percent of television shows containing violent content. Perhaps most ominously, in terms of the message transmitted to children, 38 percent of the violence is committed by "attractive perpetrators," and 75 percent of the violent acts result in neither remorse by, nor punishment of, the perpetrator. In fact, over 40 percent of the violent incidents are accompanied by humor.

Our Rabbis teach us, *There is no comparison between what we hear and what we see* (*Mechilta, Yisro* 19:9). Visual images have an impact that goes far beyond that of the printed word. Proof of this concept was illustrated when Moses came down from Mount Sinai with the Ten Commandments. He had already been informed that the Jews had made a molten calf: *They have strayed quickly from the way that I have commanded them. They have made themselves a molten calf, prostrated themselves to it and sacrificed to it* (*Exodus* 32:8).

However, it isn't until Moshe actually *sees* what is happening that he reacts by angrily shattering the Tablets: *It happened as he drew near the camp and saw the calf and the dances that Moses' anger flared up. He threw down the Tablets from his hands and shattered them at the foot of the mountain* (*Exodus* 32:19).

Moses did not respond emotionally when the information was transmitted through auditory channels. It was only after witnessing the scene with his own eyes that the full impact of what happened was absorbed. Parents should therefore be aware that the power of visually based media, such as television and computers,

---

[2] Federman, J. (1998), "National Television Violence Study III," Thousand Oaks, CA: Sage Publishing.

is far stronger than the auditory input that children receive from radio or tapes.

This insight, coupled with the surveys discussed above, makes clear that children who watch television on a regular basis are exposed to more inappropriate material than their great-grand-parents might have seen in a lifetime in the *shtetl*. While this appears to give them a veneer of sophistication, particularly in sexual matters, their knowledge is superficial. This can be mis-leading to parents who think that they do not have to engage their children in discussions on these issues. On the contrary, it is particularly important to engage children who are bombarded with the false values of the media in conversations aimed at counteracting these negative influences, by actively sharing how antithetical they are to everything we believe in.

In one of the most revealing studies on the impact of television on children, researchers intensively studied two Canadian towns that were similar in every way with one exception: The towns were separated by a mountain that did not allow one of the towns to receive any television reception. When technology advanced to the point that television was made available to this town, research-ers saw a perfect opportunity to enhance their understanding of television's effects on children. After television was introduced, children began reading less and fighting more. In general, the quality of family interaction deteriorated. I frequently see children who come from homes where there is no television, as well as children who come from more "modern," observant homes where they watch television and movies. The difference in the way these children conduct themselves is almost palpable. There is typically an air of innocence and a refreshing lack of sophistication in the more sheltered children. The pseudosophisticated presentation of the children who have been exposed to television and movies makes them seem less like children and more like pseudo-adults.

In light of the negative influences just described, it should come as no surprise that following an experimental TV blackout — when families agree not to watch television for one week — research documents cite increased family cohesiveness, longer conversa-tions between family members and heightened use of imaginative play by young children. Notice how different children's interactions are on Shabbos compared to the rest of the week. Without the distractions of television on Shabbos, parents often find that their children engage in more creative play, read more and interact more positively with parents, siblings and peers.

◀ᴣ Jewish Perspective on External Influences

The central role that Judaism places on the responsibility of parents to manage their children's relationship with the outside world goes back to the beginning of history.

The *Midrash* addresses a very fundamental question. Since the Torah is a guide for *all* time, why did Hashem wait until Sinai to give the Torah? Wouldn't it have made more sense to have given the Torah at the very beginning? After all, why not give the Torah to Adam, who was God's direct handiwork? Indeed, this is suggested by the *Midrash: Adam was worthy to be given the Torah, but Hashem decided to postpone it and give it to the descendants of Adam (Toldos Adam, Bereishis Rabbah, Parshah 24).* But why? A possible answer is suggested by the Talmud in *Chullin* (60a), which teaches us that Adam was created as an adult. He never went through a period of childhood or adolescence. The teachers of ethical values explain that this teaches us that a period of gradual growth and education is an essential ingredient necessary to master the Torah. To be exposed to the world of adulthood before going through a process of gradual development and readiness violates a central component required to prepare children for a life that truly integrates the values of Torah. When children are robbed of that crucial period of gradual development, through premature exposure to the world of adults, the foundation necessary for the internalization of Torah values is not stable enough to provide the essential scaffolding for a mature understanding of Torah's wisdom.

Neil Postman, a well-known educator, has noted that there is a little noticed, subtle effect that may accompany the exposure of children to inappropriate material that in previous generations was reserved for adults. He hypothesizes that when there are no secrets there is no shame. In a society where anything goes and everything is considered within the realm of the acceptable, children never develop a sense of productive shame. The expression *bosh panim*, shamefaced, is used by our Sages (*Ethics of the Fathers* 5:23). Latter-day commentators have suggested that this phrase should be vowelized as *bosh pinim*, meaning *inner shame*. This inner sense of shame can serve as an internal policeman, insuring that we are always on guard to protect the proper standards and values taught to us by parents and teachers. While psychologists have documented the destructive quality of the sense of damage that can accompany feelings of shame, characterized by a view that one's very character is *bad,* the teachers of ethical values have focused on the healthy component of inner shame. A diminished sense of productive guilt that can fuel spiritual and moral growth is a casualty of children's premature exposure to inappropriate external influences.

The central importance of recognizing parents' responsibility to take an active role in managing their children's exposure to the external environment is also illustrated in a lesson that goes back to the beginning of history. The Torah tells us that after Cain killed Abel, he took a wife and had a son, whom he named Enoch (Chanoch). *And Cain knew his wife, and she conceived and bore Enoch. He became a city-builder, and he named the city after his son Enoch* (*Genesis* 4:17). The question is an obvious one: What is the significance of Cain's naming his new city after his son? Cain was addressing an issue of central importance in his life. He asked himself, "How could I have done such a terrible thing — killing one-quarter of mankind?" He then came to the realization that something had been missing in his own education, and he wished to emphasize the central importance of educating the next generation. Part of his repentance for the murder of his brother involved the naming of his son Chanoch, a name related to the Hebrew word *chinuch* — education. Each time Cain called his son by name, he sensitized himself to the need to educate the next generation. Cain realized, however, that he could not educate his son in a vacuum. Teaching a child to live properly requires a proper environment outside of the home as well. Thus Cain responds to this need by building a city that he calls by the same name as his son, Chanoch, to emphasize the central importance of providing our children with an environment that will nourish proper values. Parents must take an *active* stance in protecting their children from an environment that often teaches values that are antithetical to everything that Judaism stands for. This is a central truth that goes back to the very beginning of how *chinuch* — education — was viewed by our ancestors.

The Torah addresses itself directly to our responsibility to resist the influence of the prevailing external culture: *Do not perform the practice of the land of Egypt in which you dwelled; and do not perform the practice of the land of Canaan to which I bring you, and do not follow their traditions (Leviticus* 18:3).

The commentators point out that this verse addresses itself to two components that are involved in unsavory influences of the external world — the attraction of the new and the habit of the old. The culture of Egypt *in which you dwelled* is the source of longstanding influences — some of which have been part of the environment for so long that their impact is like deeply ingrained habits that one is not even aware of. The excitement of the new — of the land *to which I bring you* — poses its own danger. The Torah cautions us to beware of the deeply ingrained influences that we have unwittingly absorbed while simultaneously standing guard against the excitement and attraction of the novel. It is also of note that the Torah uses the term *traditions* (literally, their decrees) at the end of the verse, rather than *their laws.* The term *chok* (decree) refers to a rule that does not inherently make sense. The Torah is warning us that we may feel a particular attraction to external influences that make no sense. The music, humor and holidays of secular society may be attractive precisely because their irrational qualities exert a unique pull on the attention and interest of our children, who can be naturally attracted to irrational forces. Ironically, people may feel less guilty about being sucked into irrational influences. One may embrace such influences precisely because they are not perceived as being antithetical to one's beliefs and loyalties, as compared to more rational and threatening external influences.

◄₂ Impact of Exposure to Violence

The Torah is acutely sensitive to the impact that war and violence can have on society. The importance of appreciating the impact that war has on our sensitivity to the concept of *tzelem Elokim* (the image of God) is illustrated in *Deuteronomy* where in the midst of a discussion of the laws of war in the Torah portions of *Shoftim*, continuing in *Ki Seitzei*, the text seemingly digresses and presents guidelines on how to handle the discovery of an unidentified body: *If a corpse will be found on the land that Hashem, your God, gives you to possess it, fallen in the field, it was not known who smote him* (*Deuteronomy* 21:1).

The Torah, before resuming its discussion of the laws of war, discusses how the community is to assume responsibility for dealing with a single death. Logically, the Torah should have continued with the laws of war as a theme. What is the message behind this disgression? Our Rabbis say that the Torah was concerned that, when a society wages war, however justified, the value of human life can be cheapened. The Torah, therefore, interjects the need to assume responsibility for even a single, anonymous life. After determining the city nearest to the body, the elders of that city have to declare, *"Our hands have not spilled this blood"* (*Deuteronomy* 21:7).

Rashi explains that the elders must testify that the town fulfilled its responsibility to this individual by insuring that he did not leave the city without being fed and accompanied on his way. The Torah is therefore teaching us that when, as a result of the desensitizing influence of war, we are in danger of treating life casually, we must sensitize ourselves to the value of every human being.

In contrast, American society has such a high tolerance for violence that other countries often modify the violent content of children's programming that originates in the United States before allowing these shows to be aired in their countries. During World War II, a major hurdle faced by American officers training combat soldiers was the inability of approximately one-quarter of the soldiers to kill the first time they were in combat. In contrast, during the Vietnam War there was no need to train soldiers to overcome a natural hesitation to kill. As the first major war fought by soldiers who had been born into homes with television, there was no need to inoculate them against the horrors of combat. Exposure to countless murders on television made it much easier for them to overcome such hesitation.[3] The argument is not that television makes our children into murderers. What it does seem to do, however, is erode their standards and affect their view of the sanctity of human life. The unimaginable is made all too real, and children are made to feel too comfortable with violence.

In fact, there have been empirical studies evaluating the impact of television on the homicide and assault rates in countries throughout the world. In a series of studies investigating the impact of the introduction of television on crime rates in various parts of the world, Centerwall[4] hypothesized that if television had never been introduced in the United States there would be 10,000 fewer homicides each year, 70,000 fewer rapes and 700,000 fewer injurious assaults.

> *In the early 1990's an Avianca plane ran out of fuel and crashed in the backyard of a large home on Long Island. Approximately half of the passengers survived the impact since, without fuel, the plane did not explode after the crash landing. By chance, a television news crew was in the area and arrived at the same time as did the rescue workers, who were desperately trying to free the men, women and children trapped in the wreckage. In a support group for the emergency workers that took place shortly after the crash, an emergency medical technician told of desperately trying to free a child who was trapped under the seat of his plane. It was evening, and the lights of the television camera crew were guiding him. Not*

---

[3] Grossman, D. (1996), On Killing: The Psychological Cost of Learning to Kill in War and Society, New York, Little, Brown.

[4] Centerwall, B. (1992), "Television and violence: the scale of the problem and where to go from here," *Journal of the American Medical Association*, 267:3059-3063.

knowing at the time that there was no risk of explosion, the rescue worker was desperately trying to extricate the child. Suddenly, the man holding the lights disappeared and that area of the plane became pitch black. The EMT desperately called to the cameraman, "Come back! I need the light!" The cameraman refused to come, answering, "I have a better shot over here."

Parents need to understand that what drives the television industry, including television news, is a desire for profit and the melodramatic. Parents are often lulled into the false sense of complacency that watching television news is educational and can't harm a child. In fact, research shows that children who frequently watch television news are at risk for developing what's termed the "mean world syndrome" — they develop the view that the likelihood of something bad happening to them is more than the facts support. For example, such children vastly overestimate their risk for being injured in a fire or becoming the victim of a crime.

In 1988, a devastating earthquake in Armenia took the lives of as many as 100,000 people. I co-authored a paper describing research on the psychological impact of this tragedy on the children living in the city that was at the epicenter of this disaster. The editors of the journal that was to publish the paper made its acceptance for publication conditional on the research team's explaining a very puzzling finding. The control group used in the study consisted of children living in the capital of Armenia, many hundreds of miles from the cities affected by this disaster. Yet, we found that, while not as traumatized as the children who had experienced the earthquake, they had an unusually high level of post-traumatic behavioral and emotional symptoms, even several years after the earthquake. When these children were re-interviewed it was discovered that, together with their families, they had spent the days after the earthquake glued to their television sets watching graphic footage of the earthquake on the news. Since many of these children had friends and family members in the areas devastated by the earthquake, the images broadcast on television led to their being almost as traumatized as the children who had directly experienced the earthquake.

At a time when there are many horrifying graphic images coming from Israel, it is particularly important that parents recognize that exposure to television images has far greater impact than radio news. As the principle of *There is no comparison between what we hear and what we see* teaches us, auditory input is far less powerful than when the source is also visual.

❧ Other Media: Video Games, Internet and Music Tapes

Video and computer games have some advantages over television. They are less passive and by their very nature require that a child actively engage in an activity. They have even been found to improve children's spatial skills.[5] However, parents must be aware of potential difficulties with these activities as well. Approximately 80 percent of video games contain violence as part of the game strategy, and about one in five depicts violence directed against women. Frequent playing of violent video games is associated with increased aggression in young children. Parents of aggressive children or of children with intense temperaments need to keep in mind that these youngsters are particularly prone to become more aggressive after playing these games.

In recent years, the Internet has emerged as a powerful force in many children's lives. In a recent survey, approximately two-thirds of a group of children said that they preferred surfing the Internet to watching television. The advantages of the Internet include increased opportunities, particularly for adolescents, to practice social interaction as well as its obvious educational advantages. As with television, however, there are enormous potential dangers. The risk of exposure to inappropriate material or people over the

---

[5] Villansi, S. (2001), "Impact of media on children and adolescents: a 10-year review of the research," *Journal of The American Academy of Child and Adolescent Psychiatry,* 40:392-401.

Internet is heightened when parents fail to take an active role in monitoring their children's Internet use. Some of the problems that children have encountered on the Internet include receiving multiple e-mails that take them to unsuitable sites and contact with unsavory people who can attempt to take advantage of them. Parents who are not comfortable with computers are often too passive in this area. They need to recognize the importance of familiarizing themselves with the basics of Internet use so that they can take a more informed approach in monitoring their children's use of the Internet.

Parents should be aware that in the last several decades lyrics of rock music and music videos have become considerably more explicit. As with other media, there is concern that this music can desensitize children and adolescents to violence and can also impact on their values. In fact, research has found that adolescents who prefer heavy metal and hard rock are more likely to present with risk-taking behavior, suicidal ideation and depression.[6] Mental health experts believe that the music does not cause these difficulties, but that this type of music often appeals to adolescents with this emotional and behavioral profile. Parents whose children seem drawn to heavy metal or hard rock should see this interest pattern as a possible marker for underlying difficulties.

Finally, as noted in earlier chapters, the impact of various media is, in part, a function of your child's temperament. Children with difficult, angry temperaments may be at particular risk for being negatively impacted by aggressive television shows, movies and music. As was discussed earlier, those children who have an anxious temperament need more of a protective shield than other children. They are much more sensitive to potential danger, and they are particularly likely to be adversely affected by exposure to upsetting material on television or the media.

An 8-year-old girl, with an anxious temperament, was referred because of her refusal to take a bath or shower

---

[6] Martin, G., Clarke, M. Pearce, C. (1993), "Adolescent suicide: music preference as an indicator of vulnerability," *Journal of the American Academy of Child and Adolescent Psychiatry* 32:530-535.

for close to a year. Her parents, who were unclear about the source of this aversion, were forced to give her sponge baths. The origin of her phobia, the girl eventually shared, was that her father had taken her to see an R-rated movie that very graphically portrayed a woman being murdered in a bath. Her fear was so great that almost a year after seeing the film she panicked even at the mere mention of the title of the movie.

Recommendations:

■ If you are going to allow your child to watch television, make sure that the TV is kept in a place where you can control the viewing. The number and types of shows that parents allow a child to watch in a given week need to be regulated. Parents are often surprised at how quickly even the most television-addicted children adapt to a firm set of rules aimed at reducing their television consumption. One of the most potent interventions parents can exercise is to "immunize" their child against some of the negative effects of television, by discussing issues raised in shows with controversial topics. Occasionally joining your children while watching a sitcom, for example, can present an opportunity for sharing your values on whatever issues are presented in the show. This takes a passive and possibly destructive process and changes it into an opportunity for transmitting important values.

■ Preschoolers can be particularly affected by exposure to aggression on television or in video games. Their cognitive immaturity can result in confusion as to whether the aggression they view was motivated by good or bad intentions. Even the fast pacing and short segments of *Sesame Street* have been found to be associated with increased aggression in frequent *Sesame Street* watchers.

■ Parents are frequently not aware of how tuned in their children are to prominent news stories. They may hear about the news from friends or when parents listen to news radio while driving the family somewhere. Or they may see newspaper headlines or overhear the television when the evening news is on. Children under the age of 6 can become frightened by what they see, as they have only very limited ability to recognize that news reports focus on the unusual. They perceive danger if something bad happens, no matter how rare or unlikely. Preschoolers should not be allowed to watch television news, particularly if there are no adults present to monitor the suitability of what is being discussed. Elementary-school-age children (between 6 and 12) are particularly vulnerable to the negative impact of television news. Allowing children this age unfettered exposure to television news carries the risk that they might become desensitized emotionally from responding to even the most horrifying and shocking events. This is also an age where concerns about burglaries, natural disasters, fires and kidnappings are common. These youngsters lack the perspective of older children and often hesitate to discuss their concerns with their parents. Since local news shows are particularly likely to report the events that most concern this age group, children should not be allowed to watch such shows. Parents should be particularly vigilant about allowing school-age children to watch TV news after major terrorist attacks in Israel. At such times explain what happened and talk with them about what such events mean for their own safety. Reassure your child that there are people working to make sure that their personal world remains safe. Include your children in the community's efforts to respond by saying *Tehillim (Psalms)* or through *chessed* projects for the victims.

■ Parents should monitor the type of music that their children listen to. They should familiarize themselves with the lyrics of the music, and monitor whether there are parental advisories on the CD's that their children purchase.

■ If parents are going to allow their children access to the Internet, the youngsters need to follow some basic rules. As with television, it is important that the computer be kept in a public part of the house rather than in the child's room. Children should be cautioned never to give out personal information such as their real name, address or phone number online. Online friends should never be met in real life unless the child is accompanied by adults in a public place. Parents need to monitor the places that their child visits online, as well as the amount of time spent online.

■ As with other areas of parenting, monitoring a child's exposure to external influences must be viewed in the context of the parent-child relationship. If children are living in a community where most of their friends have access to televisions and/or the Internet, then the child will likely find a way to watch television or go on the Internet in their friends' homes. The best antidote to this is a close and open parent-child relationship that fosters true internalization of the values that can inoculate children from the negative influences of the outside world.

Chapter Eight:
Peer Pressure

Feeling insecure about one's level of acceptance by peers is a normal part of childhood and it is accompanied by the need to be viewed as part of the crowd. Although such feelings are particularly strong during adolescence, younger children also have an intense need to fit in. Once one becomes an adult, it is easy to forget the anguish that can accompany the feeling of being excluded by the peer group. A recent research investigation is informative. In this brain neuro-imaging study, research participants were scanned during a virtual ball-tossing game from which they were unfairly excluded. Researchers found that the part of the brain activated when the subject was distressed due to social exclusion was the same area that goes "online" when one is physically attacked. The scientists speculate that the feelings of pain that accompany social rejection are neurologically identical to the distress experienced when physically attacked.[1] Apparently the well-known nursery rhyme *Sticks and stones can break my bones but names can never hurt me* is not accurate.

There are a number of classic experiments in psychology that highlight the powerful pull of the pressures of our surroundings. In one of the best-known studies of this process, Dr. Phillip Zimbardo converted the basement of the Stanford University Psychology Building into a setting for a fascinating study on the impact of

---

[1] "Does Rejection Hurt?" an MRI study of social exclusion, *Science Magazine*, Volume 302, Number 5643, Issue of 10 Oct. 2003, p. 290.

environment on behavior. Half of the study's participants, all of whom were undergraduate psychology majors, were assigned the role of prisoners and the other half were given the role of prison guards. Originally the study was to last for one week, but the participants' response was so powerful that after several days the study's research assistants threatened to quit unless Dr. Zimbardo terminated the experiment. The *guards* in the study became upset when they found themselves involved in sadistic and brutal treatment of their *prisoners* in spite of this being contrary to their belief system. Similarly, the *prisoners* found themselves pulled into a brutal life-style that they found inconsistent with their true value systems. This process was so upsetting to both *guards* and *prisoners* that, to safeguard their emotional well-being, the study had to be ended well before its scheduled termination.[2]

One of the most frequently raised questions is related to helping children resist peer pressure that leads to engaging in improper or destructive behavior. How can parents help their children do the *right thing* when faced with pressure from peers to deviate from the lessons that teachers and parents are trying to instill? Common questions encompass the setting of rules for one's children, when their peers' parents are more lenient. For example, can a parent reasonably limit a child's access to television or the Internet when the child's peers are allowed to go online or watch certain television shows or movies in their homes? What if parents set a strict, relatively early curfew for their child on weekend nights, resulting in a bitter complaint that he or she is being teased by peers because of having to be back home so early? Other arenas where peer pressure might be evident range from social situations where friends might incite one's child to be cruel to someone who is different, to more overtly dangerous situations, such as pressure to smoke, use drugs, or engage in other high-risk behaviors. Although dealing with peer pressure can be viewed as a lifelong process, this issue

---

[2] Zimbardo, P. G. Maslach, C. and Haney, C. (2000), "Reflections on the Stanford Prison Experiment: Genesis, Transformations, Consequences," in T. Blass (Ed.), *Obedience to Authority: Current Perspectives on the Milgram Paradigm,* (pp. 193-237), Mahway, N.J.: Erlbaum.

is probably most intense during adolescence. To better understand the dynamics of this process a brief review of the role of friends, particularly during adolescence, is in order.

As any parent of adolescents soon discovers, friendships are a major focus of their life. Making friends, keeping friends and spending time with friends will often seem more important to an adolescent than their studies or family relationships. Friends play a crucial part in the process of becoming independent from parents. The feedback and appraisals that adolescents receive from trusted friends help shape their developing identities. In a review of over 80 empirical studies investigating the role of friends in children's development, impressive evidence is presented regarding the crucial positive role played by healthy friendships in helping children grow into productive adults. This research consistently shows that social interactions with peers are core ingredients in developing a positive self-concept, ensuing school success, building effective problem-solving skills and promoting a healthy identity with parental values.[3]

What is it about friendships that can play such a positive role in your children's lives? Adolescence can be a particularly self-centered period of life. Friends are often the antidote to this self-involvement and to the loneliness that is a frequent component of adolescence. Lack of self-consciousness and a growing ability to share one's innermost thoughts and concerns with close friends make one less defensive and more open to learning. It is through friendships that children learn how to compromise and accept the views of others. The ability to do this well is perhaps the best preparation for marriage and parenting — two adult roles that call for high levels of empathy, a sense of perspective and the ability to accept flaws in others.

What are some of the negative influences of friendship? In childhood and early adolescence the main thrust is to *fit in* and be accepted. In children and adolescents who lack confidence

[3] Newcomb AF, Bagwell C: "Children's friendship relations: a meta-analytic review." *Psychology Bulletin* 117:306, 1995.

it is often difficult to *be oneself*. Psychologists who work with adolescents often find that the central fears at that stage of life are loneliness and not fitting in. The cruelty of children who are members of cliques to those outside of their group, as well as the lapse in judgment that often accompanies children's decisions to engage in risky behavior when faced with peer pressure, often stems from the volatile mix of self-doubt and this intense need to please and fit in.

In both childhood and adolescence friends tend to be similar to one another in abilities and outlook. Rejected children tend to become friends with other rejected children, and aggressive children with other acting-out children.[4] It is, therefore, not surprising that studies find that a major predictor of anti-social behavior is a situation in which an adolescent's peer network is composed of friends who smoke, drink, use drugs, or have a negative attitude toward education. Conversely, children who are attracted to friends with positive outlooks are more likely to develop positive school-related attitudes, career aspirations and achievement goals. The crucial message for parents, however, is to recognize that a normal part of growing up involves youngsters placing an increasing value on the input and influence of their peers. Consequently, to inoculate children against unhealthy forms of peer pressure requires conscious attempts to reach out to youngsters and provide them with tools to resist the pressure to engage in unhealthy behaviors.

◄ Jewish Perspective on Friendship

The psychology literature on the crucial role played by friends in child development is echoed in numerous places in Jewish sources. In perhaps the best-known statement on the pivotal role

---

[4] Fornari V. & Pelcovitz D., "identity formation in children and adolescents," in Sadock, B., *Comprehensive Textbook of Psychiatry*, 2000, Philadelphia, Lippincott, Williams and Wilkins.

friends play in a person's life, Choni Hamaagal, after a prolonged absence, finding that all of his friends have died, says, *"Either companions or death"* (*Taanis* 23a).

The Jewish perspective on friendship is perhaps best summarized in two approaches to the etymology of the word. The Hebrew word for friend is *chaver* and is derived from the word *chibbur,* which means attached or joined. It can also be seen as coming from the word *chav* — debt, or obligation. Both interpretations of the word contain powerful lessons on the meaning of friendship, as well as the approach parents need to take in educating their children about this aspect of their development.

In an enlightening insight into the *connection* component of friendship, Rabbi Dovid Fox relates the following story: He was hiking in the desert outside of Los Angeles when he came across a date ranch. When he asked the rancher to explain the process involved in managing the ranch, the latter explained that in order to produce commercially viable dates the palm trees have to be planted close together. While a palm tree growing alone will produce dates, they lack the sweetness that makes them attractive to consumers. To produce dates that are edible, the trees have to grow together, with their roots intertwined — only then can they grow in a way that will yield sweet fruit. As Rabbi Fox resumed his hike he came to understand the true meaning of the verse *A righteous person will flourish like a date palm* (*Psalms* 92:13). Connection with others is the key to living a fruitful and righteous life. A life of isolation or one lacking in knowledge about how to be a true friend will not yield the sweet fruit necessary for a full and meaningful existence.

An approach to friendship that reflects the *chav,* obligation component, is discussed by Maimonides in *Ethics of the Fathers.* Rabbi Yehoshua ben Perachyah says, *Acquire a friend for yourself* (*Ethics of the Fathers* 1:6). Maimonides explains that the reason the word *purchase/acquire* is used is to teach us that to be a true friend one has to engage in the hard work of seeing the world through the eyes of one's friend. Rabbi Yehoshua is teaching us that in relating to friends we have an obligation to relate to them not based on our needs but based on the needs of our peers. Rather than insisting that a friend meets *our* standards and expectations, friendship requires that we *purchase* this invaluable commodity through the capital of undertaking the hard work of fully relating to our friend's needs and perspective. When a child learns how to truly be a friend, he or she is acquiring the invaluable ability to relate to the different needs and views of others, from a position of respect and understanding. The lesson that friends teach a child involves accepting that we are not all the same. Learning to embrace a friend's perspective and differences and set aside our own needs and views are invaluable tools in a child's development. Friendship is about obligation, duty and giving — not about taking.

At a more basic level, parents need to teach their children that every purchase has a price. The obligations of friendship often involve the child's transcending of his or her own immediate pleasures and preferences for the sake of others. The *chav* of *chaver,* the Mishnah teaches us, requires that we *purchase* our friends by investing the time and effort to make their needs and concerns paramount.

Maimonides describes three levels of friendship:

Chaver l'daver — friendship for a thing. This level characterizes most friendships in young children. It is a friendship based on common cause — on the principle of "You scratch my back, and I'll scratch yours." Examples of this type of friendship are children who forge a bond of friendship based on enjoying the same toys, sports activities and interests, or adults whose friendships are based on business partnerships or shared political beliefs. As we learn later in *Ethics of the Fathers*, such friendships are typically short-lived. Once the usefulness of the relationship disappears the friendship is likely to end — *When the cause is gone, the love is gone* (*Ethics of the Fathers* 5:19).

2. *Chaver l'daagah* — a friendship based on concern and worry about the welfare of one's peer. In such a friendship — which typically develops in later childhood and early adolescence — one shares anxieties, concerns and sorrows. This type of friendship transcends the more superficial and ephemeral utilitarian *chaver l'daver* friendship, replacing it with a true connection marked by empathy, worry, support and love.

3. *Chaver l'dei'ah* — a friendship based on shared values and knowledge. This type of friendship is the most enduring. Just as the most successful and enduring marriages transcend the *"chaver l'daagah"* stage to encompass a shared vision of common values and goals, so too, ideal friendship involves a shared dedication to the same values and goals. In this manner a friendship transcends the narrow concerns of two people, to share a commitment to an enduring vision that goes beyond themselves.

It is interesting to note that the last of the *Sheva Berachos* (Seven Blessings recited at a wedding and at the celebratory meals in the week following the marriage) discusses the link between love and friendship — *love, brotherhood, peace and companionship.* There is an obvious connection between love and friendship and they also share a common etymology. The word love (*ahavah*) comes from the Hebrew word *hav*, meaning *give*, which is closely related to the word *chav*, the root of *chaver* (the *hei* and *ches* are interchangeable). Ultimately, the parental role in teaching children how to relate to friends is to focus on both meanings of the word *chaver*: A friend is one to whom one must connect in order to bear the sweet fruit that comes from the relationship of two human beings. Additionally, the *chav* of *chaver* teaches us that friendships require an investment of empathy, time and effort.

Although happiness in adolescence often is tied to enduring and supportive friendships, true happiness comes from resisting the pull to conformity. Parental guidance should help children resist the developmentally expected pull toward conformity and prevent them from being pulled blindly into thoughtless and self-destructive pressure. Surveys show that in spite of initial resistance, adolescents want to have discussions with their parents to help them clarify their values and what to stand up for. Even though they may initially appear to resist our input, they often integrate far more than may be apparent.

The Torah is keenly aware of the potential negative forces of the mainstream culture that can exert a powerful pressure to act against our conscience in an effort to fit in. In commanding us to avoid engaging in actions that are like those of the residents of Egypt (cf. *Leviticus* 18:3), there is a clear directive to actively reject the natural tendency to want to be like the mainstream culture that surrounds us. Ezekiel was the only one of the prophets who lived outside Israel. It is therefore not surprising that his prophecy would address the need to actively resist the seductive pull of the non-Jewish, mainstream culture. Hashem says to Ezekiel, "... *it shall not be! As for what you say, 'We will be like the nations ...'* " (*Ezekiel* 20:32). God is saying, "I will never allow you to indulge in your efforts to imitate the mainstream non-Jewish culture." We can apply the lesson of Ezekiel on the communal level to the specific of the individual. The prophecy of Ezekiel teaches us that while Hashem will not allow us to be absorbed by the non-Jewish culture, it is the job of parents to insure that their children resist the pressure to *be like the nations* on an individual level. The national appetite that Jews have to conform may be reflected on the individual level by the adolescent's drive to become part of the dominant culture around them. Whether there is an interest in the inappropriate music, dress, or behavior of the dominant American culture, parents must emulate Hashem in firmly setting the limit of *it shall not be.*

It is important to note that although children often resent initially parental guidance that steers them away from the negative influences of peers, a number of important benefits emerge over time from learning to act on the basis of one's internal compass rather than because of what others will think. Research has found that true happiness comes from acting according to one's deeply held beliefs. Although submitting to negative peer influences can result in momentary feelings of acceptance, children often find that the pleasures of belonging by engaging in risky or cruel behavior give way to feelings of emptiness and guilt. It is also of note, that in the long term the building blocks of popularity and *truly* belonging accrue from helping our children learn how to be true to themselves. In the long run, empathic, warm and kind children who don't succumb to peer pressure to exclude others are far more likely to end up being popular later in life than peers who are cruel or callous to others.

~~ Teasing and Bullying

In recent years there has been increasing recognition that parents need to take an active role in helping their children deal with chronic teasing or bullying. Teasing can degenerate into a problem that can seriously impact on our children, especially when the bully's actions become prolonged, intense, or are accompanied by threats and demands of secrecy. A brief review of some facts about this issue is presented to help parents better understand how to deal with this particularly malicious form of peer pressure.

Bullies are often children who have a temperament that is marked by poor anger control and a tendency to view even totally innocent behavior by peers as threatening or malevolent. Like many children with this temperament they frequently have difficulty seeing situations through the eyes of others and are not adept at tuning in to social nuances. Although not always the case, these children often come from homes where they are either treated harshly by one or both parents or witness frequent fighting between their parents. The parenting styles in these homes can be dominated by inconsistent disciplinary practices that alternate between harsh, overly emotional attempts to control their child and inadequate supervision. As one researcher summarized, bullies often come from homes that have an unfortunate mix of too little love and too much freedom.

What is the profile of the typical victim? The victim often does nothing to provoke an attack. They are attractive targets either because they don't defend themselves when victimized, or are easily upset and have such an intense emotional response to the attack that they give the bully exactly what he is looking for in his quest for control and recognition.

Researchers have found that while almost one out of four students (22 percent report being frequently victimized at the beginning of the school year, only 8 percent continue to be bullied by the end of the year. How do the 14 percent of children who stop being victims bring an end to the bullying? Apparently, the bully shops around for compliant victims. When a victim is too much *trouble* — either because he or she fights back effectively or enlists adult or peer support — the bully does a cost-benefit analysis and finds a victim who is easier to bother. The 8 percent who continue to be victims throughout the year have trouble responding in a way that will make themselves unattractive targets. It follows that the role of parents is to help children arrive at strategies that makes them less attractive victims.

◀ℰ Bystanders and Bullies

It is particularly important that parents understand the pivotal role played by the child who is a bystander while other children are being teased or bullied. A number of studies have found that bullying is very often witnessed by peers. Most children who passively witness an attack aren't aware how their presence often serves to subtly encourage the bully. Cruel children typically feed off an audience. While bystanders more often than not disapprove of what the bully is doing, they do not realize that they become part of the problem when they silently observe their friend's victimization and do not react. The factors contributing to this silent response include fear of being bullied themselves were they to defend their friend or a belief that the victim deserves what is happening since he is not standing up for himself. When parents help their children understand the importance of changing their response to bullying from that of a passive bystander to that of an active defender they are helping children learn the invaluable lesson of heroically resisting going along with the crowd. This lesson has the added benefit of helping a child increase his ability to resist peer pressure in other situations.

Recommendations for Helping Your Child Combat Peer Pressure:

■ At a calm time, when your children are receptive, actively discuss strategies for helping them resist peer pressure without feeling that they are being "nerdy" or "uncool." Remember that even though children may have totally internalized your values regarding appropriate behavior, these values are competing with the almost visceral need that children and adolescents have to fit in and not feel set apart from their peers. Role-play various strategies with your children that may prove helpful in finding a fit between their temperaments and workable responses. Don't be too discouraged if children are uncomfortable with role-playing, if that's not their style (or, for that matter, your style). Instead, have a direct discussion about alternative strategies for saying "No." The following list of approaches is by no means exhaustive:

- Buy time by saying "Let me think about it," or "Maybe later." While this isn't likely to provide a permanent solution, it can give your children enough distance to think in a calmer and more deliberate way about whether they really want to engage in the activity they are being tempted to do. This strategy can also, hopefully, give your child the opportunity to turn to you or another adult for advice.
- An approach that can be surprisingly effective is to encourage your child to use you as an excuse. Practice having them say phrases like, "You know how strict my parents are!" or "My parents will kill me if they find out — and they always manage to find out."
- Practice teaching your child how to say "No" effectively. The following components are the core ingredients of effectively resisting a peer's pressure to engage in inappropriate behavior.
1. Say "No" calmly.
2. Make good eye contact.
3. Resist using too many excuses. A firm "No" without explanation is often better than giving reasons that can lead to counterarguments, which may ultimately persuade the youngster to do something wrong. I (D.P.) have heard numerous times from children that, when faced with peers using cigarettes, alcohol, or drugs a simple "No" often suffices. Contrary to popular belief, many adolescents who engage in deviant behavior aren't particularly interested in tempting their peers into self-destructive behaviors. Unfortunately, they typically

have plenty of company without needing to recruit those friends who have not followed in their footsteps.

■ If your child is particularly self-confident, or is facing pressure from friends with whom he is comfortable, it might be an option to briefly present a reason without being pulled into an argument. For example, "I don't want to do that; it's dangerous," is a viable alternative, particularly when presented calmly, with confidence and with a refusal to be sucked into a futile or enticing disagreement.

■ It might be helpful to have your child accompany his "No" with suggestions for alternative, more acceptable activities.

■ The "broken record" technique can be taught to your child. Teach your child to keep saying "No" repetitively or to use another phrase repeatedly while refusing the activity (like a broken record). This approach is not appropriate for every child, but some children have been able to use this technique very effectively.

■ Accompanying the "No" by ignoring the peer's pressure or walking away can work in some situations. Although this is often difficult to implement when your child has a close relationship with the peers exerting the pressure, this option should be among those presented.

■ Parents can indirectly serve as potent models for effectively resisting peer pressure. For example, how parents handle a discussion that includes *lashon hara* (speaking ill of others) by other adults around a Shabbos dinner table can serve as the best kind of example of how to effectively resist social pressure to do the wrong thing. When children see their parents respectfully but firmly refuse to be pulled into a discussion by adults who disparage others, they are very likely to unwittingly absorb lessons that will stand them in good stead when faced with similar pressures from their own peers.

■ As noted earlier, a common issue faced by parents is children's complaints that their friends' parents allow them to engage in activities that you forbid. Remember the power of finding the balance between love and limits. While firmly reviewing the need to stick to proper codes of behaviors, in spite of outside pressures, make sure that your children feel that their point of view is heard and appreciated. As the saying goes, "To be understood, first understand." Being empathic with your children about how difficult it must be to feel that they are not fitting in can go a long way toward empowering them to resist outside pressure. Also remember that your children have to live by your rules and restrictions — they don't have to be happy about what they perceive to be unreasonable limits.

■ As discussed in earlier chapters, the best way to help your child internalize your values is in the context of a close and warm relationship. In discussing this issue remember that children will turn on their *off* button if they feel that you are lecturing, preaching, or nagging.

■ When parents are concerned about the negative influence of a particular friend of their child, they should set clear limits discouraging and, if possible, forbidding the friendship. This has to be done with sensitivity and concern about hurting the friend in question. Perhaps speak to the parents of this child to explain how it might be in the best interests of both children to discontinue their association. As noted in greater detail in the chapter on "At-Risk Adolescents (Peer Influences)," the most effective manner of accomplishing this goal is to work on increasing your child's association with more appropriate peers.

Recommendations for Helping Your Children Deal With Teasing or Bullying

■ As with other forms of peer-based difficulties, it is important to discuss a range of options with your children. When it comes to dealing with teasing or bullying one size does not fit all. A toolbox of skills that can help includes ignoring, using humor, distraction or self-defense.

■ A technique that can be used by confident children who are being teased is called *fogging*. This technique involves taking the wind out of the bully's sails by teaching your child to agree with what the teaser is saying in a manner that takes all of the fun out of the process. For example, a child who was being teased for wearing "nerdy" clothes answered by saying, "You think these clothes are strange? Wait until you see this." He then took out a picture of himself wearing even more "uncool" clothing. This brought friendly laughter from some of the bystanders and guaranteed that he was never teased for his style of dress again.

A similar approach that can be effective is to teach your child to answer every derogatory remark with the word "So?" A child who was teased by his classmates for being overweight was encouraged by his parents to answer by calmly saying "So?" As the teasing escalated he kept responding calmly with the same "broken record" response. Here too, his classmates tired of their failure to get a response and gave up on tormenting this child.

■ In some situations parents meeting with parents can be helpful. The key to making such an intervention fruitful is to calmly hear what the other parents have to say and to be respectful of their perspective. It is not unusual for such meetings to be productive, particularly if the parents of the child conducting the teasing sees this as an opportunity to teach their child proper attributes (*middos*).

■ Parents can serve as advocates for promoting an atmosphere of respect in the school. Such an atmosphere can help create a climate where teasing or bullying is not tolerated. When teachers treat children without making overly critical or derogatory comments, and when they don't tolerate children denigrating other children, an atmosphere of respect is more likely to permeate the school.

■ Be aware of how disagreement is expressed in your home between parents and between parents and children. When anger or disappointment is expressed with respect and without criticism of spouse or child, a powerful lesson on how to treat others is expressed. Conversely, children are far more likely to tease or bully their peers if they see adults — particularly parents or teachers — treating children in a critical, angry, or combative manner.

■ Parents should address the importance of not standing idly by when they see a peer being tormented. Instead of ignoring, laughing, or joining in, children can be helped to become part of the solution instead of part of the problem. The transition from bystander to *"hero"* is accomplished by helping children recognize that they are subtly encouraging the bully if they passively allow the victimization to take place. Practice strategies for assertively intervening. Parents can share the research finding that those who assertively defend their peers by standing up to bullies are often viewed as leaders and are better liked by their classmates.

PART THREE

SPECIAL ISSUES

Chapter Nine:
Helping Children Cope With Loss and Terror

The Chinese characters for the word *crisis* consists of two symbols: danger and opportunity. Parents looking for guidance on how to help their children during times of loss or instability are understandably concerned about the physical and emotional risks that may follow a death or serious illness of somebody their child loves. At the same time, periods of crisis present numerous opportunities for becoming more tuned in to what matters most in life, including making our role as parents a central priority.

In the aftermath of a family trauma such as life-threatening illness or death, or community traumas such as the terrorist attacks in Israel and the aftermath of September 11th, parents can expect a wide range of reactions in their children. Among the factors that determine the intensity of a child's response are the child's prior history of loss, the child's temperament and the intensity of parental reactions. Children may react in a number of ways to the feeling that they have lost the protective shield that they took for granted until now. Some children may express overt worries about their safety and that of family members and friends. Children confronted by the illness or death of a family member may be frightened about who will meet the needs that used to be met by a now-incapacitated or lost family member.

Sometimes the effects on children are more subtle. Such an indirect indicator may be increased difficulty in their interactions with others. If a child exhibits increased irritability, more aggression with siblings or peers, or more noncompliance in response to parental requests, parents should consider the possibility that this is an indirect child reaction to the upsetting events. Symptoms of sadness and anxiety may present in the form of vague physical complaints or changes in sleep or eating patterns. Some children may have difficulty concentrating or sitting still. All of these problems are in the realm of a normal reaction in the weeks that immediately follow traumatic events. The general guideline, however, is that if symptoms are interfering with normal functioning, particularly if they last for longer than a month, then parents should consider seeking professional help.

◄᠌ Children's View of Death

In order to understand how a child may be affected by direct loss or exposure to an event in which thousands were killed, it is helpful to review how children of different ages respond to death. Of course, infants have no understanding of death; they do, however, react to parental emotions and may respond to parental upset by becoming more cranky or clingy.

Preschoolers view death as reversible, akin to sleeping. When discussing death with preschoolers it does not take long to realize that they view death in concrete and temporary terms. In such discussions, a preschooler will tell you that people wake up in the morning, go to sleep at night, die and then get up again.

> A 4-year-old boy was friendly with an older man who lived in the apartment next door. When the man died, the 4-year-old appeared to accept news of his friend's death with relative equanimity. About six months later the man's widow told the boy's parents that their son had stopped by to ask if he could play with his friend. When the widow gently reminded the boy that his

friend had died, the boy complained: "But that was a long time ago."

The preschool years are also dominated by magical thinking; children are more likely to blame themselves for the death, imagining that it happened because of something they did.

During the early elementary school years (ages 5-9), children view death as something that can happen, but not to them. As they approach their middle school years, they gradually come to see death as universal and irreversible. Children in this age group frequently take great interest in the biological aspects of death, but are often not able to fully grapple with the emotional impact of losing somebody close to them. The capacity for abstract thought that develops in adolescence allows for a more adultlike understanding of death. Since adolescents are at an age where they are trying to figure out their place in life, death has a profound emotional impact on them. Research has shown that adolescents often have more difficulty coping with loss than they would have had in their pre-adolescent years.

Sometimes children do not appear to be obviously impacted in the immediate aftermath of the death of somebody they are close to, but later difficulties reveal a delayed reaction.

A father came to my office with his two daughters shortly after the death of their mother. After a few meetings it became apparent that this loving father and a supportive extended family were helping the girls deal with the loss of their mother without any need for professional help. Several years later the father asked me to meet with his younger daughter, who had, uncharacteristically, become a behavior problem at home and in school. After a few sessions, the following story emerged. Her teacher had told the class a story that had as its moral, "Be careful what you wish for." Her mother, who had had cancer, spent the last few weeks of her life at home, since there was little that the hospital could do for her. The morning her mother died, the girl remembers spending time in her mother's room. She sat on her mother's bed and her mother cried out in pain. The girl, who was only 8 at the time, remembers thinking, "I wish she would die already." When her mother died later that day the girl was convinced that her wish was respon-sible for her mother's death. Unable to deal with the guilt that accompanied this belief, the girl pushed the memory out of her mind until the teacher's remark, "Be careful what you wish for," triggered the unresolved guilt. Once this concern was brought into the open and the girl was reas-sured, her behavior quickly returned to normal.

◄ℓ *Child Temperament*

Some children are more vulnerable to the effect of traumatic events than others. Children who are most at risk for having dif-ficulty during uncertain times are the 15 percent of the popula-tion whose "wiring" makes them more prone to anxiety, and causes them to have greater biological reactivity to stress. When exposed to frightening events their heart rates become elevated for a longer period and they remain on the alert for danger lon-ger than their non-anxious peers. These children respond more strongly during periods of instability. They are more likely to cling to adults for reassurance and support, and have difficulty sleeping and concentrating. Although initially anxious children need more parental support than their calmer counterparts, in the long term, children with anxious temperaments respond very well to support and reassurance, and parents can expect to get their "old" child back when a sense of stability returns.

Children with Type A personalities also may respond strongly to periods of instability. Such children, who are intense and have low frus-tration tolerance, tend to have heightened cardiovascular responses to threat. They are most likely to respond to frightening events by becoming more irritable, aggressive and noncompliant. Here, too, a combination of reassurance and firm but calm limits on defiant behav-ior should lead to a quick return to pre-trauma functioning.

◄ℓ *Coping Styles*

Research and clinical practice in recent decades has found considerable variability in the coping strategies that children and adults effectively employ in coping with traumatic events in their lives. On the evening of September 11, I (DP) received an e-mail from a colleague in Israel who specializes in providing mental health intervention to survivors of terror attacks. He cautioned that in planning mental health services in New York after the World Trade Center attacks, therapists should keep in mind that the type of coping mechanism used is far less predictive of how well an individual will adjust than whether the coping strategy works for that individual.

The following vignette regarding the way a group of educators in Israel dealt with a terror attack serves as an invaluable model of how a sensitive understanding of the diverse styles of coping with tragedy can facilitate healing.

> *I (DP) was in Jerusalem shortly after a suicide bombing in Jerusalem and was asked to join an Israeli psychologist in meeting with a group of adolescents who had just lost a beloved teacher in the bombing. The school set up five rooms for the adolescents. One room was set aside for writing condolence letters to the family of their teacher, other rooms were designated for a discussion group (led by the psychologists), music, art and the saying of Tehillim (Psalms). The teens chose the room that best matched their style and seemed to find solace in finding an opportunity to deal with their grief in a manner that uniquely suited them.*

As with adults, when it comes to coping with stress in children, one size does not fit all. There is no one correct way to deal with upsetting situations. Children often deal with stress and anxiety in ways that are qualitatively different from adults. Some children may show little reaction to upsetting events. Parents should not assume that this means that their child's coping mechanisms are not working. On the contrary, a child who is showing no symptoms and is not willing to discuss the situation may be doing just as well as a child who is openly discussing his or her feelings.

Psychologists who specialize in helping children and adolescents deal with upsetting events have found the following coping mechanisms to be effective. Most people use more than one coping mechanism. Many adults and children find that over the course of time strategies that used to work best shortly after the traumatic event gradually give way to a different set of approaches.

1) Distraction Versus Confrontation:

Research on how children cope with painful medical procedures or other stressful situations finds that each child's coping style lies on a continuum from "attenders" to "distracters" — from active information seekers to information avoiders. Children who are "attenders" deal with stressful situations in an active manner. For example, if they are about to get an injection from their pediatrician they want to understand why, and they prefer to assist the doctor in preparing for the injection. In contrast, "distracter" children prefer to distract themselves when getting the injection. They are not interested in why the shot is necessary — they prefer to distract themselves by looking the other way and perhaps playing an electronic game. Interestingly, research shows that the ability to cope is compromised if one tries to turn a distracter into an attender or vice versa. For example, forcing the distracter to talk about his understanding of why the injection is necessary or forcing the attender to play a game while getting the injection will increase the child's anxiety level and he or she will cope much less successfully with the stress of the medical procedure.

This approach is echoed in two views expressed in the Talmud on how to approach worries. The verse in *Proverbs* 12:25 says, *Anxiety in the heart of a man weighs him down, but a good word makes him glad.*

Based on this verse, two views of how to deal with anxiety are discussed in the Talmud: *R' Ami and R' Assi differ in the interpretation of this verse. One rendered it "Let him banish the anxiety from his mind"; the other, "Let him discuss it with others"* (*Yoma* 75a).

The differing views of Rav Ami and Rav Assi echo the "attender" versus the "distracter" approach to dealing with anxiety. Distracters follow the interpretation of banishing the worry from their minds; attenders deal with worry by verbalizing their fears to others. In helping your children deal with the stress attendant upon loss, violence and instability, it is important to find out whether they are more comfortable using *distraction* or *attention* as the preferred approach. Specific strategies used by child psychologists consulting with pediatricians regarding how to help children during a painful medical procedure might be to have children who are "distracters" blow bubbles or play their favorite computer games during the procedure. In contrast, children who are "attenders" can be given age-appropriate reading material explaining the procedure, and can be asked to take an active role in helping the doctor prepare for it.

2) Perspective

Another powerful approach to dealing with adversity is to shift one's perspective to focus on positive changes that often come from coping with difficult situations. A study of 271 adolescent cancer survivors is typical. Of the 76 percent who viewed themselves as *different* because of the experience of coping with a life-threatening illness, 69 percent saw those differences as positive. These young men and women saw themselves as more mature, more likely to know the purpose of life and more likely to treat others well.[1]

A number of years ago, I (DP) was conducting a study of how parents react to the stress of having a child with cancer. Almost immediately after the study began my answering machine was inundated with messages from the research assistants conducting the interviews. They reported an almost universal complaint on the part of the parents of the ill children. "The questions being asked in the study only focus on the *negative* impact of our child's illness. Why haven't you asked any questions about the *positive* changes that our family experienced as a result of the experience of dealing with a life-threatening illness?" Consequently, a series of questions were added investigating the positive aspects of confronting one of the most harrowing experiences life can offer. The answers resulted in the most valuable findings of the study.

---

[1] Cited in: Stuber, ML: "Is PTSD a viable model for understanding responses to childhood cancer?" (1998), *Child and Adolescent Psychiatric Clinics of North America* 7:169-182.

The following example given by a mother of a child being treated for leukemia is a typical illustration of the study participants' view of *positive* family changes in response to coping with their child's illness.

> "Before my child was diagnosed with acute lymphoblastic leukemia the most important priority in my life was perfecting my tennis serve. About six months after my child was diagnosed, my husband was spending the evening in the hospital with my son. As I was preparing to go to the hospital the next morning, my doorbell rang. My next-door neighbor was crying. There had been a storm during the evening, and her car had been completely destroyed when a tree that was between my house and hers was felled by the strong wind. I did my best to calm her down, calling her insurance adjuster and driving her to her job. Once she entered her office I began laughing to myself. What would have happened had the wind blown in the opposite direction and destroyed my car instead? Had my car been destroyed I would have calmly said to myself, I had better call a taxi. Eventually I would have found time to fix the car. Although six months earlier I would have had the same reaction as my neighbor, my scale of priorities has now totally shifted. I know what's important in life. What's important is to be with my son and let my husband get some rest after his long night in the hospital. Material concerns mean very little to me now."

This point is elucidated by the commentary *Metzudas Dovid* on the latter part of the verse in *Proverbs* 12:25: *Anxiety in the heart of a man weighs him down, but a good word makes him glad. Metzudas Dovid* says, "But a good word means to know how to find the strength to divert this strong emotion in an effort to transpose the worry into a positive emotion by appreciating the fact that good can grow out of this experience and thus transform the worry into *simchah*, joy."

A similar message is given in a *Midrash* in *Bereishis Rabbah* on the following verse: *At that time Judah left his brothers (Genesis* 38:1).

This *Midrash* talks about a point in time — the incident of Judah and Tamar — which appeared to be a low point in Jewish history:

Joseph's brothers were busy dealing with their guilt at having sold their brother. Joseph, in his dungeon, was preoccupied with mourning and fasting. Jacob was also busy mourning and fasting in response to the loss of his son. Judah was involved in the incident with Tamar. And God [instead of viewing these events as an indication that our ancestors were in the midst of a tragic catastrophe] was busy creating the light of the Mashiach. Only God had the omniscience and perspective to know that the spark of *Mashiach,* the Messiah, was being ignited from the relationship of Judah and Tamar, and that Joseph's being sold into slavery would ultimately result in redemption.

If the typical adult has a hard time having the perspective and faith necessary to focus on the positive components of loss and trauma, one can only imagine how difficult it must be for a child. In the early stages of coping with a loss, children are typically in no position to find perspective or meaning in their experience. Over the course of time, however, as the adolescent cancer study cited above indicates, finding meaning, perspective and a focus on the positive becomes the norm — even in children.

Mental health professionals working with traumatized children have found the following questions to be helpful in assisting bereaved children to extract meaning and perspective in response to their loss. These questions are used for this purpose by a mental health team in Pittsburgh who specialize in working with children coping with the loss of a parent:

a. If you met another child whose parent died like yours did, what would you want to tell them about what you have learned?

b. What would you want them to know that might help them?

c. If they thought therapy would be too hard, what would you say to them?

---

[2] Cohen, J. and Mannarino, A., "Cognitive Behavioral Therapy for Traumatic Bereavement in Children," Center for Traumatic Stress in Children and Adolescents, Allegheny General Hospital, Pittsburgh, 2001.

d. What do you think about yourself now that you've gone through this?[2]

3) Active Problem-Solving:

Direct attempts at dealing with problems head-on include thinking of ways to solve the problem, and/or talking to others to get more facts and information about the problem.

Rabbi Samson Raphael Hirsch explains that, as Jews, we receive guidance regarding our responsibility to take an active role in dealing with difficult situations from the following verse: *He was like an eagle arousing its nest, hovering over its young, spreading its wings and taking them (Deuteronomy 32:11).* "Just as the eagle does not bear its young aloft sleeping or in a passive condition, but rather first stirs the nest up and then spreads its wings *not under but above* its nestlings, so that, with keen courageous eyes they fly up to rest on the mother's outspread wings awaiting them above ... so did God first awaken His people and get them used to have the courage to trust themselves with free-willed decision and full consciousness to His guidance."[3]

In one of the most widely cited studies regarding the powerful role of active problem-solving in helping seriously ill individuals fight illness, Fawzy and his colleagues found that teaching cancer patients effective coping mechanisms actually improved their survival rates relative to a comparison group that did not receive such instruction. Cancer patients were taught stress management skills that included learning about their illness, changing attitudes toward sources of stress by viewing them through a "new light," relaxation-training skills and systematic problem-solving skills.[4]

Of course, turning to others for support is a central coping mechanism that is essential. The healing power of *shivah* (the mourning period) is, in part, tied to the concrete evidence of social support that comes with every visit. Saying *"HaMakom"* to the mourner at the end of the *shivah* visit gives further concrete

---

[3] Hirsch, Rabbi Samson Raphael, *Deuteronomy,* 640, Judaica Press, 1976.

[4] Fawzy, Fo, Cousins, N. (1990), "A structured psychiatric intervention for cancer patients," *Archives of General Psychiatry,* 47:720-725.

evidence that the mourner is not alone — the burden of mourning is shared "among the other mourners of Zion and Jerusalem."

As King Solomon says in *Ecclesiastes: Two are better than one, for they get a greater return for their labor. For should they fall, one can lift the other; but woe to him who is alone when he falls and there is no one to lift him!* (*Ecclesiastes* 4:9-10).

In recent years, mental health researchers have gone beyond a focus on pathology to research the difference between individuals who fall apart in the face of adversity and those who seem to thrive psychologically no matter what difficulties they face. Invariably these studies find that a central ingredient in resilience is having at least one person who cares. Children facing even the worst kind of trauma and loss are buffered and protected by the knowledge that they have somebody in their corner. Such social support is a key predictor of which children will emerge relatively unscathed from even the harshest difficulties.[5]

Finding a balance between benefiting from often overwhelming levels of social support in the weeks and months following a loss or serious illness and managing to find the necessary time to be alone is among the most daunting tasks facing families struggling with the impact of trauma. Group therapists treating family members who lost a relative in the 9/11 attacks have found that among the most salient needs of the group members were requests for help in negotiating the balance between accepting social support and finding time to grieve privately. Families coping with tragedy often find that after an overwhelming show of social support in the months following a loss, the level of support available from the community often recedes, in many cases to lower levels than were available *prior* to the loss. A woman who lost a family member in a tragic accident recently told me that at times she notices people cross the street to avoid having to talk to her. The level of discomfort that others often experience when faced with tragedy may give way to avoidance, either because of not knowing the

[5] Werner, E. (1993), "Risk, resilience and recovery: perspectives from the Kauai Longitudinal Study," *Development and Psychopathology*, 54: 503-515.

right thing to say or because bereaved families can make others uncomfortable by reminding us of our own vulnerabilities.

Often, there is no "right thing" to say. Those going through a hard time may just need the feeling of support that accompanies someone's physical presence, rather than the words of friends. When Job's friends heard about the terrible tragedies he suffered they traveled long distances to offer him consolation. Yet they didn't say anything, because they realized that their physical presence was more important than words. Just being there was the type of support that Job needed: *They sat with him on the ground for a period of seven days and seven nights. No one said a word to him, for they saw that his pain was very great* (*Job* 2:13). Emotional closeness can, at times, be more effective than words. At such times words can get in the way.

Married couples often have the experience of reaching out for support from their spouses and getting a different type of response than the one needed. For example, a wife may need to have her husband listen empathically to her discussion of a problem, and the husband may respond by going into a problem-solving mode, targeting a solution to the problem rather than offering the validation and support that she is seeking. If adults have problems educating family members and friends about the best way to provide support, children will certainly need help in these areas. Parents and others can play an invaluable role in teaching children and adolescents how to effectively reach out for meaningful support from friends, teachers and other caring adults.

A team of researchers at UCLA has spent years helping adolescents around the world deal with traumatic situations such as war or disasters. They developed the following guidelines for helping traumatized youngsters reach out effectively for support.

The first part of the process is structured to help children determine what kind of support they are seeking. The following types of support have been identified by the UCLA team:
* *Emotional closeness*
* *Social connection*
* *Feeling needed*
* *Reassurance of self-worth*

- *Being there when needed*
- *Information (feedback and advice)*
- *Physical assistance*
- *Material support*

Once children identify the type of support they are seeking, the following steps should help guide them in the process of effectively reaching out to family, teachers and friends:

- Identify the person to approach
- Find the right time to ask
- Request with an "I" message
- Tell them what I am feeling
- Tell them what I need them to do
- Express sincere appreciation

Of course, these skills can be helpful to adults as well. When Dr. Laine, one of the developers of this approach, was teaching these skills to therapists working with traumatized adolescents in war-torn Bosnia, he found a totally unanticipated benefit. Many of the therapists reported that learning more effective methods of communicating their own specific support needs resulted in significant improvement in their marriages.

Self-soothing

The ability to cope with upsetting situations by soothing one's self is central to the process of successfully coping with difficult situations. This component of coping includes effort to calm oneself by praying, taking a walk, listening to music, or trying to relax.

Turning to God to answer our prayers is perhaps the most powerful form of coping. In addition to the obvious spiritual benefits, the psychological benefits of prayer include the comforting knowledge that there is something we can actively do in the face of events that are otherwise out of our control. A number of recent studies have found that prayer is associated with an improved ability to cope with painful medical conditions[6] and a positive emotional adjustment following major surgery.[7]

---

[6] Rapp, S., Rejeski, W., Miller, M., "Physical function among older adults with knee pain. The role of pain-coping skills," *Arthritis Care & Research,* 2000, 13:270-279.

[7] Ai, A., Bolling S., Peterson, C., "The use of prayer by coronary artery bypass patients," *International Journal for the Psychology of Religion,* 2000 (10), 205-220.

In a landmark study that tried to capture the essential ingredients of resilience in individuals raised in the midst of adversity, every child born on the Hawaiian island of Kauai in 1955 was followed into adulthood. Faced with high levels of poverty and abuse, one-third succumbed to the ravages of their highly stressful childhood environment, one-third were in the middle and one-third thrived. One of the key predictors of resilience in overcoming an impoverished and traumatic background was active religious observance. Those who prayed regularly were more likely to be in the resilient third that successfully beat the odds.[8] The mental health professionals conducting the study theorized that among the advantages of religious observances such as prayer were the psychological benefits of taking an active approach in the face of adversity. Active supplicants deal much better with traumatic situation as opposed to passive individuals who are like logs floating on a river, at the mercy of whatever comes their way.

Writing about the upsetting event is another powerful mechanism for self-soothing. Numerous well-designed research studies conducted over the last 15 years have found that writing about one's thoughts and feelings regarding stressful events for up to 20 minutes on each of several days can reduce illness, enhance the functioning of one's immune system, improve grades and even increase the likelihood of unemployed individuals getting a new job.[9] In one study, several hundred people with arthritis or colitis were divided into two groups. Half were asked to spend 20 minutes a day for three days writing about the worst thing that ever happened to them, and the other half were asked to spend the same amount of time writing about their daily schedule. Four months later the group that wrote about the worst thing that ever happened to them showed significant improvement in their symptoms. These studies suggest that "talking out" one's worries can apply even to one's self.

---

[8] Werner, E. (1993), "Risk, resilience and recovery: perspectives from the Kauai Longitudinal Study," *Development and Psychopathology,* 54: 503-515.

[9] Cameron, L. and Nicholls, G. (1998), "Expression of stressful experience through writing," *Health Psychology,* 17:84-92.

Diary-and journal-keeping about the experience of loss should be encouraged in older children and adolescents. Some specific guidelines that have been suggested as a focus for writing about loss include keeping a diary about memories of the lost relative. While writing about memories can cause some sadness, these feelings can be an important part of the healing process. This process also allows children to revisit happy memories that should prove to be a source of consolation. Some therapists who specialize in working with bereaved children encourage the child to make a book of memories including pictures, poems or other writings about the lost relative. Some ideas for writing about memories suggested by the childhood-bereavement specialists in Pittsburgh[10] include writing about the following themes regarding the lost relative:

- Favorite clothes
- Funniest habit
- Best time we ever had together
- Favorite things that he/she gave me
- The nicest thing he/she ever did for me
- His/her favorite expressions/jokes

Please keep in mind that the timing of these writing exercises is very individual. In many situations the child might not be ready to do this for many months after the loss. Also note that it would be counterproductive to put pressure on a child to complete these writing exercises.

Another form of self-soothing is crying. The following story illustrates this aspect of crying.

> A baby, who was being treated in the hospital for leukemia, had a particularly heartrending cry every time a medical procedure was performed on her. Although the pediatric oncology staff was used to hearing crying children, this particular child cried in a way that the parents and medical staff found very difficult to bear. The psychologist who was asked to help the parents and staff deal with this

---

[10] Cohen, J. and Mannarino, A., "Cognitive Behavioral Therapy for Traumatic Bereavement in Children," Center for Traumatic Stress in Children and Adolescents, Allegheny General Hospital, Pittsburgh, 2001.

problem hooked the baby up to biofeedback equipment that measured the baby's physiologic levels of stress as she cried. The parents and staff found great comfort in seeing that the more the baby cried, the calmer she became. This insight led to their actually welcoming the baby's cries, since they realized that this was a cry of relief and self-soothing, rather than a cry of distress.

⁂ How Parents Can Help

It might be helpful to ask children directly how well they are coping; who — if anyone — can help them; and what they have found to be most effective or ineffective in addressing their anxieties. Don't try to force a style that does not work. If children are *attenders* they will do best if allowed to discuss their concerns openly. Your role is to be honest and direct, while at the same time offering reassurance that you are doing your best to keep them safe. Children who are *distracters* will almost certainly prefer not to hear too many details about unpleasant topics. Your job is to respect their right to remain silent and try to find teachable moments when they may be more receptive to brief discussions aimed at giving reassurance and providing information. Parents whose children's coping styles differ from their own may find it hard to deal with their preferred mode of processing difficult information. One of the challenges of parenting is to recognize that we often have to let our children find their own way, even if their style of coping differs greatly from our beliefs about what works best.

Most children are resilient. If they show little in the way of obvious emotional or behavioral difficulties after traumatic events, parents should not assume that they are hiding their true feelings. In fact, researchers at Harvard, investigating the long-term psychological adjustment of children who lost a parent, found that two out of three adjusted well without the benefit of any professional counseling.[11]

---

[11] Worden, W. J., *Children and Grief: When a Parent Dies,* Guilford Press, NY, 2002.

In some cases, there may be a delayed reaction. Research shows that most parents and teachers are not aware when their children are having difficulty dealing with the impact of traumatic events. Consequently, even if children are doing well in the aftermath of tragedy, it might be advisable to occasionally check with them to make sure that there are no concerns that require clarification.

> Approximately six months after the bombing of the Federal Building in Oklahoma City, an 11-year-old girl, who lived over a thousand miles from the site of the bombing, seemed upset and preoccupied shortly before the family was to go on a vacation. In a discussion with her mother, she confided that a picture of the hotel where they would be staying reminded her of the Federal Building. She felt safe as long as she stayed near home, but the thought of staying in a place that was reminiscent of the building that had been bombed triggered fears that had remained latent until the family was leaving the safety of home. Once she was able to voice her concerns, she responded to her mother's reassurance and was able to manage her anxiety.

Creating an atmosphere that allows children to voice their hidden anxieties requires a relaxed, indirect approach. It is fine to occasionally pose such questions as, "I'm wondering how you feel today ..."; "It seems you are quiet today, I'm not sure what your thoughts are ..."; "It sounds like ...." Keep in mind, however, that parents are far more likely to engage their children in meaningful conversation about their apprehensions if the questioning is not too insistent. Although it may be difficult for parents not to be able to directly discuss upsetting issues during troubling times, parents must separate what is within their control from what isn't. It is within your control to let your child know that you are available to discuss *any* concerns. For many children it may be enough to know that you are there; active discussion is not necessarily best for them, nor is it necessarily needed at that time.

There are a few guidelines to keep in mind when children do discuss their concerns. Research on children's responses to upsetting situations consistently shows that they do better when their parents answer questions honestly and directly. Evasion in the name of protecting children tends to heighten anxiety. On the other hand, reassuring children that the adults in their life are there for them and will do everything they can to support them physically and emotionally constitutes honest discussion that validates children's concerns about the realities of facing loss, while at the same time calming their fears.

Researchers on the psychological impact of traumatic events have long noted that even the most intelligent people may have difficulty understanding and processing information about anxiety-provoking situations. Consequently it is important for parents to recognize that children's cognitive and emotional regression in response to frightening events may necessitate parental repetition regarding what happened, as well as frequent reassurance.

> *A woman whose child was being treated for leukemia made herself an expert on every aspect of her child's treatment. One day she received a call from her child's doctor saying that her son was in remission (meaning that the cancer was under control and was no longer active). Under normal circumstances she knew exactly what remission meant — but she was too paralyzed with anxiety to ask the doctor whether this meant that her child was going to live or die. Eventually she called the mother of another child being treated in the same center. Her friend reassured her that the doctor was giving her good news.*

> *Five-year-old twins were not responding to parental reassurance in the weeks following the attack on the Twin Towers. Three weeks after the attack, as her mother was putting her to sleep, one of the twins asked, "Mommy, why do people hate twins?"*

As noted earlier, when young children try to make sense of traumatic events they are more likely than older children to personalize and think in concrete terms. Consequently, they are particularly prone to misinterpret the meaning of upsetting events.

Finally, at times, parents won't know the answer to a child's question. When children ask difficult questions such as, "Why do bad things happen to good people?" it may be more comforting for the child when the parent answers, "I don't know." Sometimes children prefer parental honesty about not having all of the answers. When Aaron was told about the death of his two sons, the Torah tells us that his response was silence: *And Aaron was silent (Leviticus* 10:3).

The commentary *Ksav V'Kabbalah* asks why the Torah uses the Hebrew word *va'yidom* instead of the more commonly used Hebrew word for silence — *va'yishkot.* He answers that the Hebrew word *sheket* is used when people know something but choose not to share their knowledge. In contrast, *demamah* is a term that describes a silence that results from being truly speechless — a combination of total acceptance of Hashem's judgment and not knowing what to say.

Recommendations

■ In discussing upsetting events with children, keep in mind that good *listeners* are generally more comforting than good *talkers.* It is often helpful for parents to wait before answering a child's question, in order to make sure the child's true, underlying question is clear. If parents aren't clear about the underlying meaning of a question it might be helpful to ask the child, "What made you think of that"?

■ In dealing with adolescents, remember that even though many will not verbalize their fears, they may need to be reassured about their safety and security. In the weeks after the September 11 attack, many parents noted that teens who had previously felt comfortable being home alone asked that their parents stay home with them at night.

■ It is particularly important to monitor childhood exposure to the media in the aftermath of terrorist attacks. Young children, in particular, may respond to each television replay of the Twin Tower attacks as if they were happening for the first time. It is also important to supervise young children's exposure to upsetting pictures in newspapers or news magazines. Also, keep in mind that children may be affected by repeatedly hearing adult discussions about the impact of the attacks.

- Helping children take an active role in response to traumatic events is often therapeutic. Some of those who lost family members in the crash of TWA Flight 800 reported that the only comfort they found in the days following the crash was in looking at the hundreds of drawings that children from around the country sent them, offering their condolence. Encouraging children to help raise money or to send letters of support to families that lost members in the attacks provides an opportunity for them to take an active role and teaches them important values that can act as an antidote to feelings of helplessness.
- Studies of children who lost their fathers in the Yom Kippur War found that their mothers' ability to speak of their sadness in front of their children played a crucial role in the children's recovery. Parents should therefore feel comfortable occasionally discussing their sadness and concerns with their children. If this is done in a way that conveys a sense of loss mixed with reassurance and hope, children will learn a valuable lesson about dealing with upsetting situations.

Chapter Ten:
The At-Risk Child*
Implications and Interventions for Parents in the Orthodox Jewish Community

In recent years there has been an unfortunate increase in the number of adolescents from observant Jewish families who have been seriously disruptive, rebellious and defiant. This chapter will define the nature and scope of the problem, discuss some hypothesized causes for such difficulties, as well as provide a summary of recommended interventions for parents.

◄◊ Definition

The term "at-risk" refers to a set of difficulties with parents and/or school that an adolescent may experience in complying with the rules of home, school and community. Using the common yardstick typically employed in the field of child mental health, these difficulties will be defined as meeting the criteria for "at-risk" only when the adolescent crosses the threshold into behavior that causes significant distress in the adolescent or his

---

* This chapter is based in part on a monograph published by Dr. David Pelcovitz for Azrieli Graduate School of Jewish Education at Yeshiva University, 2005.

other family, and are also accompanied by significant levels of impairment in the adolescent's functioning. Specific examples may include:

- A reduction or absence of religious observance relative to the accepted norm of observance expected by home and school.
- Drug or alcohol use or abuse.
- Defiance of parental rules that leads to significant parent-adolescent conflict.
- School truancy.

⊷ Scope of Problem

The insular nature of the Orthodox community, as well as the sense of shame that typically accompanies this problem, makes it very difficult to get a handle on the true scope of the at-risk problem. In the most comprehensive survey of the incidence of at-risk behavior in the Orthodox community, the Metropolitan New York Coordinating Council on Jewish Poverty conducted a study[1] of the scope of the problem in the Brooklyn Orthodox Jewish community. Their methodology was a survey of 25 Brooklyn-based organizations that work with Orthodox youth, including schools, hot lines and mental health professionals who work with adolescents in the community. Based on this approach, the researchers concluded that Brooklyn's 23,000-student yeshivah system includes approximately 1,500 at-risk 14–17-year-olds. These adolescents were found to be engaging in "serious" at-risk behavior, including theft, substance abuse, truancy and running away from home. The study's authors acknowledge that limitations of their methodology would bias their results in a manner that significantly underestimated the scope of the problem. They estimate that an additional 2,500 adolescents are engaged in similar behavior but have not been identified. It is important to note that while the conclusions

---

[1] Metropolitan NY Coordinating Council on Jewish Poverty Survey.

Danziger, Y. (1999), "The incidence of at-risk youth in Orthodox Jewish community of Brooklyn, NY." Report to the New York City Department of Youth and Community Development, Metropolitan Council on Jewish Poverty.

of the study reflect a higher than expected incidence of at-risk adolescents in the Brooklyn Orthodox community, the estimates are approximately half of the estimated incidence of similar difficulties reported in the general population of Brooklyn.

◢ℓ *Clinical Presentation*

In the Orthodox Jewish world, when does it cross the line into at-risk behavior? Nefesh, an international organization of Orthodox mental health professionals, held three two-day conferences to arrive at a consensus as to how to define and approach the problem of at-risk adolescents.[2] Each of these conferences was attended by approximately 70 invited experts — rabbis, parents, outreach workers and psychotherapists who have worked with this population in the United States, Canada, England and Israel. The conferences resulted in three editions of a manual that outlined the attendees' consensus regarding identification, prevention and intervention for the troubled adolescents and their families. Although subject to the obvious bias inherent in any definition of a problem arrived at by consensus, the following expert consensus definition emerged regarding the presentation of the at-risk adolescent in the Orthodox community:

Soft Signs: Generally in a 13 to 14-Year-Old
Changes from typical behavior within his/her community
  • The music listened to has changed.
  • Not learning well; great impatience shown with academics.
  • Language is changing, with greater usage of slang.

Medium Signs: Generally in a 15 to 16-Year-Old
  • She/he will be in her/his second yeshivah by the sophomore year.
  • Smoking cigarettes.
  • Beginning to have family conflict.

---

[2] Russell, S. and Blumenthal N. (Eds.), "Children in Crisis: Detection and Intervention: A practical guide for parents and mental health professionals." Nefesh, the International Network of Orthodox Mental Health Professionals, New York, 2003 (Third Edition).

- Symptoms of sexuality are out of the norm for his/her community.
- Change in clothing and hairstyles.
- May not have used marijuana but knows the language of the drug culture.
- Consistently downs a few shots of whisky or beer at kiddushim.

Hard Signs: Generally in a 16 to 19-Year-Old
- Is a chronic truant or a dropout.
- He/she is no longer following any rules of the house; conflict with parents is routine; conflict spills over into relationships with siblings, and parents will worry about the effect on their other children.
- Attending parties without parental knowledge or permission, going to clubs, or partying at friends' houses while the parents are on vacation — therefore the house is empty for a few days.
- Spending an excessive amount of time out of the home.
- Use of marijuana and/or other drugs.
- Stealing may be commonplace.
- The observance of Shabbos, *kashrus* and *Tefillin* are, for the most part, dropped.

◄ Risk Factors

Perhaps the only agreement among those who work with this population about the cause of at-risk behavior in Orthodox adolescents is that such difficulties can rarely be attributed to a single source. Among the most prominent hypothesized causes is the existence of any persisting condition that makes an adolescent feel marginalized and not accepted by family, peers or society. It is logical that in such situations the adolescent seeks a sense of solace and belonging by finding similar-minded peers who pull the adolescent into deviant behavior. In recent years, organizations such as Priority One, a Long Island-based organization that specializes in reaching out to at-risk Orthodox youth, have conducted weekend retreats for families and professionals struggling with this issue. A major component of the weekend is a panel made up of a group of adolescents and young adults who are either currently engaging in at-risk behavior or who have overcome their difficulties and have returned to the mainstream. The focus of these sessions is a discussion of the basic reasons for their rebelliousness. What is striking is that although there is a wide variety of reasons for their rebellion perceived by the adolescents, the common thread that consistently runs through their narratives relates to **feelings of alienation and exclusion**. Whether their inability to feel connected stems from a history of academic failure, abuse, intense conflict with parents, or spiritual alienation, these youngsters were not able to connect with role-models who could help them feel part of their family, school, or peers. These panelists consistently described finding such feelings of belonging only when among similarly alienated friends.

Biological and Genetic Factors

A growing body of evidence has documented that, particularly in situations where serious behavior problems have an early onset, biologically driven and/or genetic influences can play an important role in placing a child at-risk for significant behavioral difficulties in adolescence. For example, adoption studies have found that serious conduct problems in children, particularly those that include aggressive behavior, have a strong genetic component that interacts with environmental influences.[3]

Recent research has found that children who present with early onset behavioral difficulties often have subtle deficits in the frontal part of the brain.[4] The frontal lobes, the foremost region of the brain, have been found to be involved in key personality traits ranging from affect regulation to capacity for empathy and ability to self-monitor. The following behavioral difficulties all involve functions served by the frontal regions of the brain:

[3] Cadoret et al., 1995. R. J. Cadoret, W. R. Yates, E. Troughton, G. Woodworth and M. A. Stewart, "Genetic-environmental interaction in the genesis of aggressivity and conduct disorders." *Archives of General Psychiatry* 52 (1995), pp. 916-924.
[4] Greene, R. (2000), *The Explosive Child:* A New Approach for Understanding and Parenting Easily Frustrated, Chronically Inflexible Children. New York, HarperCollins.

- Difficulty shifting from one mind-set to another, inability to flexibly shift from one strategy to another in problem-solving.
- Organizational deficits which may lead to difficulty in areas of anticipating problems, formulating goals in response to problems, selection and evaluation of appropriate responses.
- Deficits in working memory (e.g., child blurts out answer because otherwise he will forget what he wants to say).
- Problems with goal-oriented planning.
- Difficulty self-monitoring.

Of course, biology is not necessarily destiny. With proper support from family and school, such children can learn to overcome these executive functioning deficits, in spite of their dysregulated temperament. However, when parents and teachers are not able to effectively teach the child how to override this predisposition, he or she is at increased risk for becoming a member of the next generation of at-risk adolescents.

◀ℓ Emotional Correlates

Attention Deficit Hyperactivity Disorder (ADHD)

The above-described difficulties are often part of the constellation of symptoms seen in children with ADHD or other children presenting with seriously disruptive behavior. In fact, recent research using neuroimaging techniques have found subtle abnormalities in the frontal portion of the brain in children diagnosed with ADHD.[5] The inattentiveness, low-frustration tolerance and high-activity level that are core ingredients of ADHD have been found to be highly correlated with increased risk for significant behavioral difficulties in adolescence. In fact, it is estimated that a child with ADHD is 10 times more likely to be diagnosed with serious behavioral difficulties.[6]

---

[5] Tannock, R. (1998), "Attention Deficit Hyperactivity Disorder: Advances in cognitive, neurobiological, and genetic research." *Journal of Child Psychology and Psychiatry*, 39, 65-99.

[6] Angold, A., Costello, E. and Erkanli, A. "Comorbidity." *Journal of Child Psychology and Psychiatry and Allied Disciplines* 40 (1999), pp. 57-87.

When children present with a combination of ADHD and significant conduct problems, they need to be followed very carefully since the "double trouble" of ADHD plus behavioral disorders places them in a pool of children at particular risk for more pervasive and serious behavioral difficulties in adolescence. This high-risk group of children is also more likely to develop significant difficulties with anxiety, impaired self-concept and aggression.

In the only systematic study of ADHD in at-risk Orthodox Jewish adolescents, Feldman[7] found that a group of 24 at-risk Orthodox adolescents scored significantly higher than a comparison group on a standardized measure of ADHD. Almost one-third of the at-risk adolescents in this study were found to present in a manner that was highly suggestive of a diagnosis of ADHD.

Oppositional Defiant Disorder (ODD)

Oppositional defiant disorder is a psychiatric diagnosis which, as outlined in the diagnostic manual used by the mental health profession,[8] is characterized by a pattern of frequent negativistic, hostile and defiant difficulties that lasts for at least six months and causes significant impairment in the child's ability to function well at home, in school or with peers. This pattern of behaviors is characterized by some or all of the following: frequent loss of temper, argumentativeness with adults, an active defiance or refusal to comply with adults' requests or rules, repeated attempts to deliberately annoy people, a tendency to blame others for his or her mistakes or misbehavior. Such children are also often described as touchy, resentful and easily annoyed by others. They may respond to anger at others by becoming spiteful or vindictive.

ODD is more likely to be predictive of risk for later severe conduct problems when characterized by high levels of severity and persistence (Cohen et al., 1993). In one study, when children met criteria for ODD in their preschool years, almost 70 percent

---

[7] Feldman, A.D. (2004), "Parenting style and behaviors associated with attention deficit/hyperactivity disorder (ADHD) in at-risk adolescents in the Orthodox Jewish community," Unpublished manuscript.

[8] American Psychiatric Association (1994), *Diagnostic and Statistical Manual of Mental Disorders*, 4th edition (DSM-IV). Washington, DC: American Psychiatric Association.

were presenting with more serious behavioral difficulties by age 9 (Campbell, 1991). In addition to early onset and symptom severity, specific symptoms have been found to be of particular concern. For example, researchers determined that when pre-adolescents present with frequent fighting, cruelty to peers, or running away, they are particularly likely to develop more severe conduct problems as adolescents.[9] These researchers conclude that a particularly ominous predictor is when these children present with aggressive behavior that is premeditated, rather than part of an angry, impulsive outburst.

Parents should keep in mind that those children with ODD who also have ADHD are more likely to develop more serious behavioral difficulties as they grow older. When ODD presents without the accompanying inattentiveness, impulsivity, or high-activity levels of attention-deficit, there is lower risk for later serious behavioral problems.

Depression and Withdrawn Behavior

A number of studies have found a strong connection between delinquency and depression. A review of the studies investigating the depression-conduct-problem connection concluded that as many as one-third of adolescents with severe conduct problems are clinically depressed and up to an additional 50 percent have been found to have milder forms of depression.[10] At-risk adolescent girls are particularly likely to suffer from significant levels of depression.[11]

The depression-conduct disorder link is a particularly important one for parents to be aware of. Because of the often silent nature of child and adolescent depression, it is typically difficult for parents to be aware of significant levels of depression in their

---

[9] Loeber, R. Burke, J., Lahey, B. Winters, A. and Zera, M. "Oppositional defiant and conduct disorder: a review of the past 10 years, Part I." *Journal of the American Academy of Child and Adolescent Psychiatry* 39 (2000), pp. 1468-1484.

[10] Vermeiren, R. (2003), "Psychopathology and delinquency in adolescents: a descriptive and developmental perspective." *Clinical Psychology Review,* 23 (2003) pp. 277-318.

[11] Ulzen, T. and Hamilton, H. (1998), "The nature and characteristics of psychiatric comorbidity in incarcerated adolescents." *Canadian Journal of Psychiatry* 43 (1998), pp. 57-63.

child. The earlier depression is diagnosed and treated, the better the long-term prognosis. When parents get their depressed child help before the problem blossoms into a full-blown depressive disorder they can save their child from suffering long-term difficulty in controlling their moods and behavior.

Shyness and self-consciousness tend to protect children from risk for later behavioral difficulties.[12] Understandably, a temperament characterized by fear of others and anxiety about new situations makes it less likely that an adolescent will be pulled into the novelty-seeking behavior that typifies many adolescent delinquents. In contrast, children who are socially withdrawn and present in a manner that combines low levels of anxiety, a low need for approval from adults and a preference for being alone may be at increased risk for developing significant behavioral problems as adolescents.

◀‿ Family Factors

There are a number of factors that have been found to be associated with families that have an at-risk adolescent. Although not exhaustive, the following variables have been found to be associated with increased likelihood of disruptive behavior in adolescence:

Disciplinary Style:

Researchers have consistently found that a parental discipline style characterized by high levels of emotionalism, criticism, lecturing or physical punishment is associated with an increased chance that a child will be noncompliant and rebellious.[13] Additional risk factors include parental inconsistency, particularly if accompanied by failure to adequately monitor one's child's activities outside the home.

---

[12] Kerr M, Tremblay R., Pagani L, Vitaro F. (1997), "Boy's behavioral inhibition and the risk of later delinquency." *Arch. Gen Psychiatry* 54:809-816.

[13] Loeber, R., Hay, D. (1997), "Key issues in the development of aggression and violence from childhood to early adulthood." *Annual Review of Psychology*, 48:371-410.

[14] Sharp D, Hay D., Pawlby S., Shmucker G., Allen H., Kumar R. (1995), "The impact of postnatal depression on boys' intellectual development." *J. Child. Psychol. Psychiatry* 36:1315-36.

Attachment Problems Between Parent and Child:

When parents' emotional difficulties get in the way of their ability to establish a secure attachment with their child, the risk for later behavioral difficulties increases. For example, when a parent is depressed during a child's early years, the child has an increased risk for presenting later with aggression and disruptive behavior.[14] There are likely multiple determinants underlying the parental depression/child-conduct-problem connection. Since irritability is often a component of depression, depressed parents are more likely to respond to a child's misbehavior in an unproductive, emotional manner. Furthermore, the pessimism inherent in depression makes it more likely that there will be a focus on the negative in the child's behavior. Such children may come to think that they can't win, since any efforts at improvement are squelched when their depressed parent fails to recognize these attempts.

Parental Powerlessness

When financial problems or high levels of marital conflict deplete a parent's emotional resources, they are often not able to place appropriate limits on their children's behavior. Research has consistently shown a strong connection between such parental difficulties and subsequent behavioral difficulties in their children.[15]

Favoritism Toward Siblings

Children who feel that they are not loved and appreciated by their parents, particularly when they feel that a sibling is consistently favored, are more likely to develop behavioral difficulties. For example, a team of psychologists researching this issue found that older siblings who felt that their behavior was unfairly controlled as compared to younger siblings, whom they perceived as being treated more leniently, were more likely to engage in disruptive behavior.[16]

---

[15] Pelcovitz, D., Kaplan S., "Child witnesses of violence between parents: Psychosocial correlates and implications for treatment." *Child Psychiatric Clinics of North America* 1994; 3:4 745-758.

[16] Dunn J., Stocker C, Plomin R., (1990), "Nonshared experiences within the family: correlates of behavioral problems in middle childhood." *Developmental Psychopathology.* 2:113-26.

In the earlier-cited study of 24 at-risk Orthodox Jewish adolescents, Feldman found that the adolescents in the comparison group were more likely to describe their parents as using an authoritative disciplinary style characterized by striking an ideal balance between appropriate limits and sufficient warmth and love. This finding suggests that the literature regarding the difficulties experienced by parents of at-risk adolescents is applicable to the Orthodox Jewish family as well.

Parental Interest in Child's School Performance

Parents who take an active interest in a child's performance in school and are able to create a partnership with teachers in maximizing their children's academic potential are more likely to raise children who do not develop serious behavioral difficulties.

◄ε History of Abuse or Trauma

Research on abused children and adolescents consistently documents significantly increased risk for disruptive behavior disorders and substance abuse.[17] Although there is no systematic research documenting the abuse-at-risk connection in the Orthodox Jewish community, there is ample anecdotal evidence to support such a connection. The insular nature of the Jewish community, coupled with an accompanying reluctance to report abuse to secular authorities, may have led to an exacerbation of the abuse problem in a community that otherwise has numerous protective factors (e.g., community support, religious restrictions) against the possibility of child abuse.[18] A presentation at an Orthodox Jewish conference on the at-risk problem (Nefesh-Ohel Conference on Children in Crisis, 2000) included a symposium with a number of presentations that anecdotally documented the high rate of undisclosed sexual abuse in at-risk Orthodox adolescents.

---

[17] Kaplan S., Pelcovitz, D., Salzinger, S., Weiner M., Mandel, F.S., Lesser, M.L., and Labruna, V.E., (1998), "Adolescent physical abuse: Risk for adolescent psychiatric disorders." *American Journal of Psychiatry*, 155(7), 954-959.

[18] Pelcovitz, D., (1998), "Identifying the abused child: The role of day school parents." *Ten Da'at* 2:9-11.

⁇ Academic Achievement

In the last several decades there have been a number of studies that have shown that poor school achievement increases risk for later serious behavioral difficulties. In one study researchers found that poor school achievement in first grade increased risk for disruptive behavior in elementary school and predicted a "delinquent personality" by age 14.[19] Language difficulties have been singled out as having particular import in predicting later behavioral difficulties. A number of studies have documented the importance of early identification and remediation of verbal deficits as core ingredients in helping prevent vulnerable children from developing at-risk behavior as adolescents.[20]

Academic difficulties play a particularly crucial role in the genesis of behavioral difficulties in yeshivah students. The central importance the Orthodox community places on education, coupled with the greater demands of the curriculum and the lower tolerance of children who don't fit the mold, are among the forces that can fuel rebelliousness in the child who encounters failure in a yeshivah. In the only systematic evaluation of the association between academic difficulties and behavior problems in the Orthodox Jewish community, Goldberg[21] investigated the association between reading problems and behavior problems in 77 fifth-grade boys attending modern Orthodox elementary schools. Consistent with previous literature, Goldberg found a significant relationship between reading and externalizing behavior problems. Of particular interest was his finding that feelings of social exclusion were part of the process feeding the behavioral difficulties in the youngsters with reading difficulties in Hebrew. Given the central role that reading Hebrew plays in the academic

---

[19] Tremblay, R., Masse, B., Perron, D. (1992), "Early disruptive behavior, poor school achievement, delinquent behavior, and delinquent personality: longitudinal analyses." *Journal of Consulting and Clinical Psychology,* 60, 64-72.

[20] Henggeler, S., Schoenwald, S. and Borduin, C. (1998), "Multisystemic treatment of antisocial behavior in children and adolescents." New York, Guilford Press.

[21] Goldberg, S. J. (2004), "The Relationship between English (L1) and Hebrew (L2) reading and externalizing behavior amongst Orthodox Jewish boys." Ph.D. Dissertation, New York University, Steinhardt School of Education.

success of yeshivah students, Goldberg's finding suggests that core academic deficits may contribute to a child's feeling set apart from peers in a manner that can fuel disruptive behavior.

◀ℓ Peer Influences

Association with deviant peers is clearly associated with increased risk for problem behavior in adolescence. Researchers have found that when exposed to peers who also engage in rebellious behavior, children are more likely to engage in substance abuse, delinquency and aggression. In one of the most comprehensive and longstanding studies of the roots of delinquency ever undertaken, the Cambridge-Somerville Youth Study followed adolescents at-risk for delinquency who attended a summer camp that exposed them to other troubled adolescents. These youngsters, as opposed to a comparison group that received no such exposure,[22] were found to have suffered numerous negative effects over the next 30 years of their lives, including increased risk for divorce, early termination from school and job difficulties.

In light of the central role played by deviant peers in promoting the development of delinquent behavior, it is not surprising that therapeutic intervention aimed at disengaging adolescents from associating with delinquent peers, while simultaneously increasing their association with conventional well-behaved peers through such activities as organized athletic events or youth groups, has been found to significantly decrease problematic behavior. For example, in the most carefully documented treatment for delinquent adolescents, therapists teach parents how to better monitor their children's activities and encourage them to better familiarize themselves with their children's peers. Simultaneously, unpleasant consequences are established for continued association with deviant peers. When par-

---

[22] Dishion, T., McCord, J. Pouling, F. (1999), "When interventions harm: peer groups and problem behavior." *American Psychologist,* 54, 755-764.

[23] Huey, S., Henggeler, S., Scott, W. (2000), "Mechanisms of change in multisystemic therapy: reducing delinquent behavior through therapist adherence and improved family and peer functioning." *Journal of Consulting and Clinical Psychology,* 68, 451-467.

Chapter Ten: The At-Risk Child / 163

ents are successful in disentangling their children from these negative influences, enduring improvement often follows.[23]

❧ Community Support

There is a clear connection between the quality of a neighborhood and children's risk for serious behavioral difficulties. Research has found that neighborhoods that have a strong sense of community are less likely to experience significant behavioral difficulties in their youth.[24] The process by which tightly knit communities exert this type of positive influence includes such activities as adults monitoring the spontaneous public social gatherings of adolescents, coupled with a willingness to intervene when they see truancy or adolescents engaging in wild behavior. In a survey of 343 neighborhoods in Chicago, significantly lower levels of violence was found in communities populated by adults who felt a sense of collective responsibility for the young residents of their neighborhoods.

In light of the above, it is not surprising that experts who work with the at-risk problem of Orthodox youth have informally noted increased risk in neighborhoods that aren't cohesive. For example, relatively higher rates of serious adolescent behavioral difficulties have been noted in large communities where a child's absence from regular attendance at *shul* is not noticed. In contrast, communities that are cohesive enough to take note of a child's absence from services, or where a child's acting-out behavior is addressed by caring adults, provide the input necessary to prevent small behavioral difficulties from degenerating into more serious rebellious behavior.

❧ Female vs. Male At-Risk Behavior

In recent years researchers have documented an increase in the number of girls who exhibit significant levels of antisocial behavior.[25]

[24] Sampson, Robert J.; Raudenbush, Stephen W.; Earls, Felton (1997), "Neighborhoods and violent crime: a multilevel study of collective efficacy." *Science,* 277, 918-924.
[25] Molidor, C.E., "Female gang members: a profile of aggression and victimization." *Social Work* (1996), 41:251-257.

In the Orthodox community there are a number of unique difficulties facing Orthodox girls who are at-risk. There are fewer alternative schools for these girls, making it more likely that if their behavior leads to expulsion from a yeshiva high school they will be further marginalized from the community by being forced to attend public schools. Since girls in the community are more likely than boys to present with behaviors that may elude early detection — such as eating disorders and depression — their behavior might not lead to identification and referral until later than is the case with boys.

◄₹ Jewish Perspectives

In the last *mishnah* of Tractate *Sotah* we read:
"In the period preceding the coming of the Messiah insolence will increase and honor dwindle; youth will put their elders to shame, the old will stand up in the presence of the young, a son will revile his father, a daughter will rise against her mother ... and a man's enemies will be the members of his household ... A son will not feel ashamed before his father" (*Sotah* 49b).

Relating this *mishnah* to the current epidemic of rebellious behavior, Rabbi Matisyahu Salomon points out that while the current situation is perhaps among the darkest circumstance of *galus* (exile), the *mishnah* also contains a message of hope. It implies that the seeds of redemption are contained in this darkness, which is part of the process that will ultimately produce the light of redemption.

The *mishnah* that was just cited ends with the following statement: *So upon whom is it for us to rely? Upon our Father Who is in heaven.* The *Netziv* understood the meaning of this statement in a unique way. According to his interpretation, the *mishnah* teaches us that when we deal with our children passively by saying that their behavior is all in God's hands we are abdicating our role as responsible parents. Of course, in raising children we have to turn to Hashem to ask for guidance and help, but ultimately the responsibility is in our hands to do everything that is in our power to expect proper *derech eretz* (respect) from our children.

As noted earlier, a major force that can contribute to a child's rebelliousness is a parental disciplinary style marked by extremes. Parents who are either overindulgent or excessively harsh are more likely to raise rebellious children. The connection between overindulgence and defiant child behavior is well illustrated in the story of King David's son, Adonijah: *All his life his father had never saddened him by saying, "Why do you do this?"* (*I Kings* 1:6). The *Midrash Rabbah*, referring to this verse, points out a number of instances where parental indulgence resulted in child rebellion, including the defiant behavior of Ishmael, Esau and Absalom — all of whom, the *Midrash* says, were not adequately disciplined by their fathers (*Midrash Rabbah, Exodus* 1:1).

Of course, the other extreme, excessively harsh parenting, is equally problematic. Rabbi Shlomo Wolbe, in warning of the dangers of such parenting, quotes Rabbi Chaim Volozhiner as saying:

> "Today, harsh language won't be accepted ... someone whose nature is not to speak softly, and who angers quickly when people don't do his will, is exempt from the mitzvah of admonishment. This is the rabbinical decision — an angry person can't admonish" (Planting and Building, p. 37).

As noted earlier, another major influence in the shaping of adolescent rebelliousness is the impact of exposure to deviant peers. The *Midrash Tanchuma (Shemini, Siman* 11) relates a fascinating story regarding the psychology of exposure to negative behavior: A man was ashamed by his father's behavior when he drank too much wine. One day, the son saw an inebriated man lying on the street while the neighborhood children taunted him and threw rocks and dirt on him. Assuming that his father would be motivated to stop drinking when he saw this humiliating scene, the son escorted his father to witness firsthand the degradation that can accompany too much drinking. To the son's dismay, his father's reaction was to go to the drunk and ask him where he could buy such potent wine for himself.

From this *midrash* we see that instead of learning a lesson from the degradation of the drunk, the person who has a weakness and an inclination to alcoholism is blinded to the negative and shameful consequence of drunkenness. Instead, he puts his own spin on the scene unfolding before him, and it's his own pleasure and thirst that is primary, preventing him from learning and changing his way of life.

While common sense dictates that children would learn to avoid rebellious behavior when they see the anguish that such behavior typically brings to the lives of their rebellious peers, it is human nature to be even further drawn into the temptations rather than recognize the consequence of negative behavior. This insight clearly supports the repeated research findings regarding the strong magnetic pull that negative peer influences have on the development of adolescent behavioral difficulties.

◄ᴈ Interventions

Early Identification

Primary prevention of at-risk behavior in Orthodox adolescents has as its cornerstone the identification of children at greatest risk for later difficulties **before** such vulnerabilities blossom into more serious and intractable behaviors. The most effective prevention efforts would involve early identification and intervention by parents in areas of difficulty that present in the following individual and family areas:

a. Individual Factors:

The biologically vulnerable child: As noted earlier, children with impulsive temperament are at increased risk for later at-risk behaviors. Early identification and intervention by a professional, particularly for children diagnosed both with ADHD and oppositional defiant disorder (ODD), are warranted. Particular attention should be paid when these dually diagnosed children live in a family environment that is either extremely chaotic or rigid.

Academic vulnerability: Children with early reading problems and/or language difficulties are at particular risk. Parents should note that, at times, such difficulties are subtle and do not emerge until the increased demands of higher grade levels bring them to the fore.

Depression: Untreated depression is a common pathway to serious behavioral difficulties in the future. While the glaring and overt nature of disruptive behaviors is easy for parents to identify, the often silent nature of depression is far easier to miss. Parents should keep in mind that depression may primarily present as chronic irritability, negativity and sensitivity. In addition, children who have difficulty enjoying themselves or who are prone to focus on the negative may also be manifesting subtle signs of a pervasive mood disorder. It is also important to keep in mind that underlying depression often co-occurs with disruptive behaviors.

Parents should be aware of how depression might present during different developmental phases. Preschoolers might present with a somber appearance, lack the bounce of nondepressed peers, make frequent negative self-statements and show tearful and spontaneously irritable behavior far more frequently than their nondepressed peers. In school-aged children, depression might present with frequent irritability and a tendency to hate themselves and everything around them. Although depression may present without a full-blown manifestation of the following syndrome, symptoms of a major depressive episode as defined by the diagnostic manual used by mental health professionals are as follows:

- Five or more of the symptoms listed below during the same two-week period, at least one of the symptoms must be either a depressed mood or loss of interest or pleasure.

1. Depressed or irritable mood most of day, nearly every day.

2. Diminished interest or pleasure in all, or almost all activities, most of day, nearly every day.

3. Significant weight loss when not dieting or weight gain (change of more than 5 percent of body weight in a month) — in children consider failure to make expected weight gains.

4. Insomnia or hypersomnia nearly every day.

5. High levels of restlessness or the opposite — a sense of being slowed down, described by adolescents as "moving through water." This must be present nearly every day, and must be serious enough to be noticed by others.

6. Fatigue or loss of energy nearly every day.

7. Feelings of worthlessness or excessive or inappropriate guilt nearly every day.

8. Diminished ability to think or concentrate or make decisions.

9. Recurrent thoughts of death (not just fear of dying), or recurrent suicidal ideation without a specific plan, or attempt.
- Clinically significant distress or impairment in major area of functioning.
- The depressed mood is not a by-product of substance abuse or physical illness.
- The depression is not related to a recent bereavement (longer than two months, or marked impairment).

b. History of Past or Current Abuse:

As noted earlier, many adolescents who present with at-risk behaviors in high school later disclose that their feelings of alienation, anger and isolation have their roots in undisclosed abuse. Although far from comprehensive, the following behaviors have been noted by experts and should trigger suspicions on the part of parents as to the possibility of abuse:

Sexual Abuse:
- Sexual behavior or knowledge which is unusual in a yeshivah setting.
- Child forces sexual acts on other children.
- Fear or avoidance of a specific place or person, such as sudden change in child's willingness to go to gym or swimming pool.
- Extreme fear of being touched; e.g., unwillingness to submit to physical examination.
- Excessive guilt, self-blame, sense of being damaged.
- Refusing to talk about "secret" he/she has with an older child or adult.

c. Family Factors:

Parental disciplinary style: Risk is increased whenever parenting relies on a rule structure that is dominated by extremes that are either overly permissive or overly strict. Both extremes on the emotional connection continuum are also of concern; parents that are either so overprotective that children feel smothered, or emotionally cold and disconnected parents. Additional concerns should be raised if there is a parenting style marked by inconsistency, a vacillation between neglect and high levels of emotionalism marked by yelling or excessive criticism.

High-conflict divorce or severe marital conflict: Risk is particularly high in the early stages of a divorce, when parents often become so preoccupied with the emotional devastation that typically accompanies the first few years of a divorce that they have little energy left for their children. Exposure of children to either interparental physical violence or the emotional abuse that accompanies marital fighting has been found to have a particularly strong association with children and adolescent behavioral difficulties.

Parental depression or other serious mental illness: As noted earlier, such difficulties can seriously compromise parents' ability to provide their children with the stability that provides the foundation for adequate behavioral control.

Ongoing family stress: Economic stress, particularly when other children in a class come from economically advantaged homes, can be a correlate of child behavioral difficulties. Similarly, other ongoing stressors in the family that can increase risk include frequent relocation, children who are first-generation Americans, or families where members suffer from life-threatening medical conditions or chronic disabilities.

❧ Environmental Factors — School and Community Climate:

As noted earlier, a sense of living in a caring community where children are valued and respected as contributing members of their family, school and community is a crucial buffer against serious at-risk difficulties. Researchers have documented a number of variables that are associated with establishing a school climate that is conducive to reducing antisocial behavior.[26] These include:

- A predictable, fair, calmly administered and consistent set of rules.
- A curriculum that is perceived by students as relevant.
- Teachers who make time for their students.
- A strong and effective principal.

---

[26] Hawkins, J. and Lam, T. (1987), "Teacher Practices, Social Development, and Delinquency," in J. D. Burchard and S. N Burchard (Eds.), *Prevention of Delinquent Behavior* (pp. 241-274), Newbury Park, CA: Sage.

• A perception on the part of the students that they have some input into the educational process.

Of course, the above "wish list," once implemented, does not guarantee an absence of serious rebellious behavior on the part of students. However, schools that provide a safe, warm and nurturing environment are more likely to temper a student's rebelliousness in a manner that can ultimately lead to a turnaround in their feelings of alienation.

Recommendations

General Guidelines

Once a child is already presenting as overtly rebellious it is important for parents to keep in mind that, since the key dynamic underlying such behavior is feeling alienated and set apart from the mainstream, parents can play a pivotal role in helping a child or adolescent feel connected. Perhaps the most potent antidote to feeling angry and alienated is feeling appreciated and understood. When parents make harsh or belittling remarks or treat a child in a manner that the child perceives as unfair, the downward spiral that the child is already caught up in can be accelerated. Conversely, a combination of time, support and understanding can go a long way toward setting a rebellious adolescent on the path toward reconnecting to more productive and meaningful behavior. The following recommendations can be considered:

1. A rebellious child does best with the balance between love and limits advocated in earlier chapters. Research indicates that consequences that work best with disruptive children and adolescents are:

• Brief, unemotional, clear, consistent and not overly harsh.
• Stemming logically from the misbehavior and make sense to the child.
• Viewed as being delivered in the context of a child feeling liked and appreciated, in spite of the punishment. When a parent shows that he or she doesn't take the child's misbe-

havior personally and disapproves of the behavior — and not the child — consequences tend to be far more effective.

A parent once pointed out to me that he always wondered why his child bristled at the slightest criticism from either parent but was able to take even the toughest and most demanding direction from the coach of his basketball team. It was explained to the parent that when children know that everybody is on the same team, they will accept even the most demanding set of rules willingly. They are most likely to rebel when they feel that their parent or teacher isn't on the same team.

2. A set of strategies that can be used to guide parents in dealing with disruptive children has been developed by Greene[27] at the Harvard Medical School. These include:

- Develop a perspective that sees the child's behavior as coming more from the child's wiring rather than from willful misconduct. Most of these children have their behavioral difficulties fueled by neurological factors or stressors that make it difficult for them to regulate their effect. While this does not mean that limits and consequences are not necessary, it does mean that the parent can respond as calmly as he or she would to any misbehavior that is coming more from a child who "can't" rather than from one who "won't" behave properly.
- Respond to children before their behavior reaches an unacceptable peak.
- Anticipate and modify situations which will likely trigger defiance by cuing in to specific factors that fuel explosiveness.
- Use of distraction, logic and empathy may work if employed before meltdown.
- Choose only worthy battles.
- Address recurring patterns by identifying specific situations that routinely cause significant frustration.

3. Whenever possible, address the spiritual. Rebellious adolescents often describe feeling alienated from spirituality, yet,

---

[27] Greene, R. (2000), *The Explosive Child: A New Approach for Understanding and Parenting Easily Frustrated, Chronically Inflexible Children*, New York, HarperCollins.

at the same time, yearning for greater spiritual understanding and connection. An at-risk child who returned from a summer program that emphasized spirituality through growth in ethical values explained the reason for the dramatic improvement in his behavior after the summer. "Until now," he explained, "I never knew who God was. God was always about what I could *not* do — don't watch TV on Shabbos, don't go to inappropriate movies, etc. Nobody ever told me who God was until this summer. Now that I understand what God is about, Judaism makes more sense to me, and for the first time, I'm interested in what Judaism has to offer."

4. Promoting effective parent-school partnerships are an essential part of any program for addressing the needs of at-risk children. Research has consistently shown that at-risk children do better when they perceive their parents as being actively involved in their education. Parents who overtly support teachers, monitor homework assignments and grades and support extracurricular school activities are sending a clear message to their children about the importance of school and of showing proper *derech eretz* (respect) to teachers. Teachers can help promote this type of partnership by providing parents with regular feedback regarding children's academic and behavioral progress, and by scheduling parent-teacher conferences in a manner that is flexible enough to accommodate parents' work schedules.

5. Expelling a child from a school should be considered only as an extreme step when *all* alternatives have been exhausted. Yeshivos that have a low threshold for expelling rebellious adolescents have unwittingly exacerbated the problem for the entire community by creating a growing group of such children on the streets, thereby fostering the kind of "deviancy training" that can contaminate more mainstream adolescents in the community. Some alternatives to expulsion that have been successfully implemented in various communities include alternative schedules, such as providing adolescents with a modified program that allows them to work for part of the day and attend school for part of the day. This allows these adolescents to remain part of their peer group and find success in nonacademic areas of strength where

they are more likely to achieve. Some schools have experimented with "exchange" programs where they "trade" a disruptive child in one school for a disruptive child in another school. When children are given a totally fresh start in a new school, they often experience success that isn't possible in an environment where they are perceived by parents and peers as troubled. Finally, although many high schools frown on early graduation, when rebellious adolescents are allowed to graduate after their junior year, they often thrive. Success can come as a result of a number of factors, including being given a fresh start in an environment where they aren't viewed in a preconceived way, being given the opportunity to make more appropriate friends and benefiting from the greater academic flexibility present in post-high-school environments.

6. Parents should be aware that in recent years a growing number of alternative schools and programs have become available to service at-risk adolescents. The principal of your child's current school, or your rabbi, should be able to help you identify the best school for your child.

Mentoring

Perhaps the most common intervention promoted by the Orthodox community, targeting the at-risk problem, is the implementation of various types of mentoring programs. Mentors are often recruited naturally in the course of a typical adolescent's life. In a study of 770 adolescents, Zimmerman, Bingenheimer and Notaro[28] found that most of the teens in their study had naturally occurring mentors and that those who did were less likely to engage in delinquent behavior, used marijuana less frequently and had more positive attitudes toward school. What are the ingredients identified by adolescents as being particularly helpful in such naturally occurring relationships? When asked what they found most helpful about such relationships, teens report that the opportunity to spend time with somebody who respected them

---

[28] Zimmerman, M., Bingenheimer, A. and Notaro, P., "Natural mentors and adolescent resiliency: a study with urban youth," *American Journal of Community Psychology,* Vol. 30, No. 2, 221-243.

and made them feel heard and supported was at the core of what they valued most about the relationship.

In recent years, in recognition of the need to service at-risk adolescents in the Orthodox community, a number of mentoring programs have been established. An example of site-based mentoring is the "Clubhouse" in London. It is a drop-in center where protégés are provided with opportunities for recreation as well as for building mentoring relationships that have a vocational education component, typically related to jobs in the area of computers, a medium that many at-risk adolescents find inherently interesting. Another promising on-site program is Bridges, in Queens, New York. This program, which is unique in that its focus is on elementary school-age children, is an after-school homework center that provides students who fall in the risk categories described above with homework support from high school students who are trained to be mentors as well as tutors. School-based mentoring programs such as TOVA, on the south shore of Long Island, provide well-trained and supervised mentors who come to schools several times a week and meet with the youngsters, providing either tutoring or a break. These mentors often meet with children off-site approximately once a week as well. School-based programs offer the advantages of both convenience and advocacy for the student by the mentor. While there are no systematic efforts, as yet, to measure the efficacy of these programs, word of mouth has provided strong anecdotal evidence of their positive impact. Parents should note that such programs do not drive a wedge between parent and child by replacing them with an alternative parent; on the contrary, research and experience clearly indicate that such relationships typically serve to improve the parent-adolescent relationship.

Conclusions:

The Orthodox Jewish community has a number of significant strengths that can be harnessed to help this troubled population. The strong value placed by the community on family and community cohesiveness coupled with a tradition that promotes concern for the welfare of children are powerful forces that likely account for the relatively lower prevalence of this problem in many Orthodox communities. On the other hand, unique stressors in the community such as the financial and emotional stresses that can accompany the raising of large families, and the strong stigma that the community places on academic weakness, are two forces that can serve to amplify risk. Parents, as well as the community, can play a pivotal role in combating this problem. The community has a responsibility to combat the stigma and rejection that often haunt these children. Research has repeatedly confirmed that the core ingredient in predicting which at-risk children are resilient in the face of multiple risks is the ability of parents as well as members of the community to continue to connect with these alienated children. Parents who continue to show love to their child, in spite of their often outrageous behavior, can begin a process that gradually helps that child recover from feelings of alienation, pain and anger.

Chapter Eleven:

Respect

In traditional books about parenting there is generally very little attention paid to the importance of respect. In Torah circles, however, *honor and respect due to parents, teachers and elders* is generally recognized as a core value that we want to transmit to our children. Still, as in so many other areas related to parenting, if we carefully examine personal relationships, we will find that modern society and culture have impacted upon the traditional observance of these major *mitzvos* and have affected our attitudes and practice, as well as the atmosphere of the Jewish home, family and community.

There are three areas that we will discuss. The first is the quality of *honoring one's father and mother.* What is the perspective of Torah regarding the values that we want to impart to our children regarding their obligations to relate to us in a spirit of respect, love and concern? The second area deals with the relationship of students and teachers and the conflicts and tensions which may exist between parents and teachers. We will also discuss the need to position parents and teachers in their proper roles so that children will get a consistent message regarding the need to show proper respect to *both.* Finally, we will address the importance of *respect for the older generation,* and the question of the extended family in today's modern society, with emphasis on the presence, or lack of, transmission of these values from one generation to the other. Respect for one's peers is discussed in the chapter on peer pressure.

There is a general consensus on the part of most adults today that there has been a breakdown in the structure of adult authority. In a recent national survey, 82 percent of adults said that the children of this generation are less respectful of adults than was the case in previous generations. A psychologist, who recently interviewed a group of adolescents in an attempt to better understand why they cut their high school class, found that the most common reason given by the adolescents was, "Who are you to tell me to go to class?"

There are a number of possible sources for this breakdown in basic respect. Perhaps the most powerful contributors are repeated portrayals in the media of adults as weak, ineffective and immoral. For example, a recurring theme in many television comedies is that of the "all-knowing" child who is far wiser and more competent than adults, who are portrayed as incompetent, ineffective and unable to control their children. Portrayals of authority have been compromised in the political arena as well. Imagine how different were the lessons about respect for adult authority for children who came of age during the media coverage of the President Clinton-Monica Lewinsky scandal compared to the sheltering of the children of the last generation by editors' and reporters' discussions to ignore similar indiscretions by President Kennedy.

The impact on our children is clear: Adult authority is something that can be questioned. The automatic assumption that children inherently know that they must treat parents with respect has been transformed into an issue that needs to be actively addressed by parents. A father who was having a hard time teaching his defiant children to be more respectful told me (DP) about the following incident that served as a turning point in achieving insight as to how to be more effective in commanding respect from his children.

> I was doing my reserve duty in the Israeli army when I overheard the following discussion between an officer and a private. The officer told the private that he had to sweep the floor in their base's dining room. The private, who was having a bad day, lost his temper and defiantly

told the officer, "You can't make me sweep the floor!" The officer calmly responded: "You're right, I can't make you sweep the floor, but I can make you wish that you did." The private immediately followed the order and cleaned the floor immaculately.

The parent-reservist who saw this interchange gained a powerful insight into how to wield authority and instill respect. When he returned from his reserve duty he began calmly and firmly telling his children whenever they were defiant, "I can't make you listen, but I can make you wish that you did." This new approach led to a significant improvement in the father's ability to relate to his children in a manner that established his authority more effectively.

Our Sages were very sensitive to the quality of honoring of one's parents. The Talmud in Tractate *Kiddushin* stresses the *how*, not just the *what*, of paying honor and respect to a father and mother. Their point of view is summarized in a pithy statement of Avimi, who states, "*One may feed his father pheasants (a delicacy), yet this [act] drives him from the world; whereas another may make him (his father) grind with a mill, and this [act] brings him to life in the World to Come*" (*Kiddushin* 31a).

The Talmud teaches us that in itself, financial support given by adult children to their parents is not considered fulfillment of the mitzvah of honoring parents if it is done without sensitivity and consideration. On the other hand, a son or daughter may not give financial support to his/her parents, but more than compensate for the lack of expensive gifts and monetary support with love, time and concern.

We may well ask ourselves: What are we supposed to bring to our parents? In the *Book of Psalms* we find a beautiful chapter picturing the Jewish home. King David states, "*Your wife is like a fruitful vine in the inner chambers of your house; your children shall be like olive shoots surrounding your table*" (*Psalms* 128:3).

This verse is somewhat difficult to understand considering the use of a mixed metaphor. First the wife is referred to as a fruitful vine, and then the children are compared, not to the fruit of that vine, which would be grapes, but to olive shoots! We may well find the answer in a story in Chapter 9 in the *Book of Judges*, in which Yosam, the son of Gideon, relates a parable regarding leadership. He depicts the trees in the forest in search of a king, as they go from tree to tree and extend an invitation to accept the position of leadership. They come to the olive tree and ask him to become their king, to which the olive tree answers, "Should I leave my fatness by which God and man are honored, and go to hold sway over the trees?" In other words, it has a far more important mission to fulfill by bringing forth olives, from which oil is produced, thus bringing honor to God and to man. The trees then come to the vine, and invite the vine to become their king. The vine replies, "Should I leave my wine which cheers and gladdens God and man, and go to hold sway over the trees?" In other words, it too has a purpose; that is, to produce grapes from which wine is made, which, in turn, brings joy and happiness to the world.

From this parable we see that wine is symbolic of joy and happiness, while olive oil is symbolic of honor. This explains why the verse in *Psalms* compares the wife to a vine, and the children to olive shoots. Parents are meant to create an atmosphere of joy in the home, while children are charged to bring honor to the family. Have we not perhaps reversed these roles? Somehow we have been taught, or have absorbed from our society, the idea that a child has but one purpose in life, and that is to bring *nachas*, joy, pleasure and happiness to his parents, while parents are supposed to bring great honor to their children so that they will be able to be proud of the position and status their parents enjoy in the community. We learn from this verse that the opposite is true. The wife is compared to a vine, because the purpose of parents is to create a Torah home, the essence of which is transmitted, not simply through discipline and authority, but in a spirit of joy and happiness. It is hoped that their offspring will be imbued with a similar sense of joy and happiness, and will be motivated to establish their homes in the same manner. It is not enough for children, on the other hand, to be simply a source of *nachas*. Rather, they must conduct themselves in a manner that will bring honor to their parents, and not, God forbid, dishonor. In this sense, we have indeed neglected the basic concept of honoring parents, by failing to understand our primary purpose of bringing honor to them. Perhaps, they, in turn, have also failed in their role and purpose of bringing *simchah* and joy to the Jewish household. Far too often there has been the harsh imposition of the parent's will and authority, unrelieved by a spirit of happiness.

It is also important for parents to understand how respect can be nurtured. As we look at the Ten Commandments we observe that they are recorded in two vertical columns, with five commandments on each side. According to some commentaries, the commandments should be read not only vertically, but horizontally as well. This means that there is a connection and relationship between the first commandment and the sixth, the second and the seventh, etc. The fifth commandment, *Honor your father and mother,* is placed opposite the tenth commandment, *You shall not covet.* There is a significant lesson in the juxtaposition. It teaches us that the honoring of parents is somehow linked with the prohibition of coveting that which belongs to another. Children are aware of what their parents wish for, what values they live by and what their objectives in life are. If parents covet money, power and position, then a clear signal has been given that they consider these things to be important in life. The children, in turn, will model their lives accordingly. When children reject the shallowness of their parents' values it can happen, sadly, that the respect that they owe their parents is compromised as well. If parents, however, pursue the goals of Torah and *mitzvos,* then their children are given a powerful lesson. They will pursue the same path and thereby pay proper respect to their parents.

The second area of honor and respect for teachers is one that should focus on the relationship not only of students and teachers, but also on the interaction between parents and teachers. In Torah circles, there is very often tension and conflict between these major molders of children's minds. The Talmud in Tractate *Bava Metzia* 9:2 teaches us, *If one's father and one's teacher have both lost articles of value [and the son has a limited amount of time to look for these articles], the loss of the teacher takes precedence [over that of his father].* A great teacher of ethics gave this *halachah* a most interesting and telling interpretation. He said that when the Talmud speaks of the teacher's *loss* and the father's *loss*, it is not only referring to an *article* that has been lost. Rather, what the Talmud says is that the rebbi's *loss*, as opposed to the father's, refers to the definition of the word *loss*. What does a person consider a loss? A father may feel that if his son does not graduate from college, or become a professional, or join him in business, a great loss has been incurred. The rebbi, on the other hand, may feel that the greatest loss is incurred when the student who has great promise does not utilize his God-given intellectual gifts to pursue the study of Torah for many years and plumb the depth of its wisdom. Instead he uses his skills in other areas which, in the eyes of the teacher, are not as important as learning Torah. In other words, the father and teacher may have a different scale of priorities, and therefore different expectations as well. The question posed by the Talmud is which of these two losses should a person consider of paramount importance. The Talmud gives its answer, and tells us that in this case the teacher's view is to be preferred over that of the father.

Certainly not every parent can accept this perspective. It is essential, therefore, for both the parent and the teacher to be sensitive and understanding of the other's viewpoint. The ultimate decision will have to be made by the student, but hopefully the process of arriving at a decision can be reached in a climate of cooperation between the yeshivah and the home, rather than in an atmosphere of conflict.

That the expectation of a father are different than those of a teacher is nothing new. Strangely, it is often the teacher who is more tolerant and understanding of the potential of the student, as opposed to the father, who may be more demanding. When Jacob blesses his children before his death, he addresses his firstborn son, Reuben, and is quite critical of him: *Waterlike impetuosity — you cannot be foremost, because you mounted your father's bed; then you desecrated Him Who ascended my couch* (*Genesis* 49:4). Jacob is critical of his firstborn son and disappointed in him as well. Yet, when Moses, our teacher, blesses the tribes of Israel prior to his death, he encourages Reuben and says to him, *May Reuven live and not die* (*Deuteronomy* 33:6). Here, Reuben's descendants are told that they are worthy of

God's blessings and that they have an important role to play in the Jewish nation. Moses, the teacher, is kinder and more understanding than the father, and this may be true in many cases to this day. A parent finds it difficult, at times, to accept the fact that his little boy or girl has grown up and is now worthy of recognition as an adult. It takes maturity on the part of the parent to appreciate that the child has now become a full-fledged adult.

It is important for us, however, to understand that both parent and teacher are unique and have different blessings to offer the son/student. The father may be more demanding and more critical at times, but he also may have a deeper understanding of his son's talents and limitations, and therefore may be capable of challenging his son in a manner that is not possible for a teacher.

On the other hand, the teacher can be more objective, and therefore more tolerant, and may detect abilities in the student that are not appreciated by his parents, who think of him far too often as a child rather than a young man. Fortunate is the one who is able to synthesize the influence of parents on the one hand, with that of the rebbi on the other hand, for each has so much to offer him.

Since differences between teacher and father in the areas of values and expectations may occur, it is important that the conflict and tension between the two be consciously reduced. Parents must be very careful not to create a climate of disrespect toward the rebbi regarding the values that the school is trying to teach. The yeshivah, on the other hand, should avoid undermining the authority of parents and must take care to foster honor of father and mother at all times. Tension between these two forces is not necessarily negative, nor mutually exclusive. What we must aim for is the *right* kind of tension to enable the son/student to benefit from *both* of these influences.

Our third area of discussion relates to respect for our elders. I (RP) was once told by a man who lived through the Holocaust that he finds that those who did not experience this historic tragedy cannot truly appreciate the greatest loss resulting from this horrendous crime against humanity. He said that it is not only the fact that so many Jews were killed and so many major Jewish communities were decimated that is devastating, but that, in his opinion, the greatest tragedy lies in the fact that a whole generation was denied the privilege and experience of having grandparents. The members of the post-Holocaust generation were deprived of a *Zeida* and *Bubba* who could impact on their lives as they grew up. What is even more disquieting, however, is the fact that so many American Jewish families have denied themselves this experience by choice. To a great extent we have witnessed the disappearance of the extended family in our society. A generation ago it was not uncommon to find a set of parents and grandparents — or if there was only one person surviving, a *Zeida* or a *Bubba* — influencing the development and maturing process of children and grandchildren in the home. Can we possibly measure the advantage and benefit that children derive from being exposed to grandparents? Can we possibly appreciate how much is denied them when they are deprived of this experience? Far too often this is the case because we are more concerned with conserving our own convenient, comfortable lifestyle. It is not only a question of lack of *respect or honor* when the older generation is taken care of by strangers, but it also means denying ourselves the opportunity to enrich the atmosphere and the climate of the Jewish home. The future depends on transmission, and transmission is realized not only through teaching in the formal sense. Transmission is also affected by the atmosphere. Our elders, by their very being and presence, strengthen credibility, trust and confidence in the past, which, in turn, is transmitted to future generations. To a certain extent we may be guilty of squandering this great resource of the wisdom and the accumulated experience and insight of older people. There is a graying of America. People are living longer and are active longer, and it is wasteful not to take advantage of their years of life experience and their wisdom and deny it to a younger generation. A wit once said that we have sadly arrived at a time where we ask our young people to give us their opinions and we tell our older people to go out and play. This may account for the success of retirement villages, but it is certainly not the Jewish way.

The Torah teaches us, *You shall rise in the presence of an older person and you shall honor the presence of a sage* (*Leviticus* 19:32). A society in which older people are respected and honored and their advice is solicited is a healthier society — one that will successfully transmit historic values to future generations as well. The Torah states this succinctly and forcefully in the verse, *Ask your father and he will relate it to you, and your elders and they will explain it to you* (*Deuteronomy* 32:7).

In recent years, a number of studies in fields ranging from psychology to sociology have documented the extensive benefits that children derive from close contact with grandparents. These studies find that children who feel close to their grandparents are better adjusted than children who do not have this important benefit.[1] Of particular interest is the fact that grandparents have been found to play a particularly powerful role as transmitters of the family's religious values.[2] In a world where many parents worry about their children's religious values and level of observance, an often overlooked resource is the powerful influence that grandparents can have — not only as a unique source of advice, love and support, but also as particularly effective religious mentors.

Perhaps most significantly, research has repeatedly documented that children living in families where their parents are under significant economic, work, or marital stress fare much better when they have close relationships with grandparents. In such situations grandparents serve as an essential source of stability and support, providing essential buffers and sources of love and connection that stressed-out parents may be unable to provide.[3]

We have touched upon three areas of *respect:* honor for parents, for teachers and for our elders. Each deserves our careful attention and examination to ensure that the quality and honor

---

[1] Lussier, G.; Deater-Deckard, K.; Dunn, J.; and Davies L., *Journal of Family Psychology,* September 2002, Vol. 16, No. 3, 363-376.

[2] Kopera-Frye, K. and Wiscott, R. (2000), "Intergenerational Continuity: Transmission of Beliefs and Culture." In B. Hayslip Jr. and R. Goldberg-Glen (Eds.), *Grandparents Raising Grandchildren: Theoretical, Empirical and Clinical Perspectives,* pp. 65-84, New York: Springer.

[3] Kennedy, G. E. and Kennedy, C. E. (1993), "Grandparents: a special resource for children in stepfamilies," *Journal of Divorce and Remarriage,"* 19, pp. 45-68.

we pay them meet the standards of Torah. These standards are admittedly most demanding and are at times difficult to meet. Nonetheless, we ignore them at our own peril. A social commentator once said many years ago that we must turn away from the soft vices by means of which a society can decay, and return to the stern virtues by means of which a strong society is made. And this must be done because reasonable men know that in the final analysis the hard way is the only enduring way. How true this is of the *mitzvos* (precepts) of honoring father and mother, paying proper respect to our teachers and extending the deference due to our elders. By pursuing the "hard way," in the areas we have discussed, we will retrieve these beautiful *mitzvos* and insure that they will be constantly observed and treasured, for they certainly represent the cement of a decent and meaningful society and guarantee a productive and fruitful future for ourselves and for our children.

Recommendations:

- When a child is disrespectful to a parent it is understandable that the parents may respond with a combination of hurt, anger and indignant attempts to obtain respect. Unfortunately, such a response almost guarantees that children and parents will get sucked into an escalating spiral that will seriously interfere with the process of teaching them how to relate to their parents in a more respectful manner.

- A more effective parental response is to deal with disrespectful children in a calm but firm manner. Recognize that while you may have no control over the immediate situation, you do have control over the long-term consequences. The first step in responding to a child's *chutzpah* (insolence) is to refuse to be pulled into their circle of anger and defiance. Instead, pull back both emotionally and physically by telling yourself that to respond in kind is to miss the opportunity to teach the child the importance of honoring one's parents. When both child and parent calm down enough to engage in a calm discussion about how inappropriate and hurtful his or her disrespect is, you can discuss the consequences of his or her actions. What often work best are logical consequences that are meted out *measure for measure*. For example, not driving a child to a friend's house, or, in the case of older children, having them do their own load of own laundry can be a valuable reminder that parents are constantly doing things for their children that require gratitude and respect. Keep in mind that calmly delivered short-term, reasonably limited consequences (e.g., insisting they do one load of laundry as opposed to making them do the laundry for one month) that make sense to the child are more likely to be effective than more draconian measures.

■ Children are far more likely to relate to adults in a respectful manner if they see their parents relating to each other with respect. The ultimate lesson in *respect* is imparted when, on a daily basis, a child sees his parents communicating with one another with deference, parenting in a manner that values the other parent's views on how to raise children and disagreeing with each other in a calm and respectful manner.

■ Webster defines the word *respect* as "to treat with special consideration or high regard." The Hebrew word *kavod* is based on the word *kaveid* — something that is weighty, of significance. Children are taught to treat adults respectfully when *they* are treated with "special consideration" and viewed as "significant" individuals. On a practical level this means talking to our children in a manner that does not belittle them and confers value on their point of view. Respecting their privacy by knocking on their door before entering their room, not eavesdropping on their conversations or opening their letters helps permeate the home with an atmosphere of respect.

■ Parents should never criticize a teacher in front of their children. There is a difference between empathically hearing a child's concerns about problems in school and crossing the line into overtly siding with a child against a teacher in a manner that conveys a lack of respect. Be aware that children often overhear parents discussing concerns about school or shul in, what adults think, are private conversations. Research shows that adults often underestimate how aware children are of adult discussions and attitudes. Also keep in mind that children absorb lessons about the importance of *respect* from seeing how we treat strangers. Every time we treat a cab driver, cashier, or waiter with patience and politeness, our children absorb a valuable lesson about respect for others.

■ Children should be taught to appreciate their grandparents' (and elders') wisdom, experience and insight. It is a good idea to act as a model by showing appreciation for your own parents' advice and support. When you show respect for your parents, your children learn how to respect you as well.

Chapter Twelve:
Self-Esteem

Any book on parenting needs to recognize the central role that nurturing a child's self-esteem plays in raising a well-adjusted child. Research in psychology has repeatedly documented that a healthy sense of self-worth is an essential building block for a life of happiness and success.[1] Conversely, when a child develops a pervasively negative view of himself, he is at increased risk for living a life plagued by depression, eating disorders, occupational failure and victimization by others.

◄ፄ Jewish Perspectives on Self-Esteem

Any discussion of the Jewish approach to instilling a positive self-concept in children must first deal with an obvious question. How does one reconcile the strong emphasis that Jewish tradition puts on humility and modesty with the emphasis that psychology places on enhancing a child's self-worth and importance? The following Talmudic passage is but one of many examples of the emphasis placed by our Sages on the importance of humility: *Rava said, "It [the Torah] is not in the heavens" (Deuteronomy*

---

[1] Bednar, R. L. and Peterson, S. R. (1995), *Self-esteem: Paradoxes and Innovations in Clinical Theory and Practice* (pp. 96-117), Washington, DC, American Psychological Association.

30:12) ... neither will it be found in one who believes his mind is as broad as the ocean — it [the Torah] is not to be found with the person who, because of some level of Torah knowledge, is overly expansive in his self-esteem as the sea. *R' Yochanan said: "It is not in heaven"* — it *[the Torah] is not to be found among the arrogant (Eiruvin* 55a).

In fact, the Talmud in *Sukkah* (29b) explains: *The sin of arrogance is equivalent to all [the others]; in contrast, regarding the humble it says: "But the humble shall inherit the earth"* (*Psalms* 37:11).

Rabbi Aharon Kotler, *zt"l* (of blessed memory), stresses the crucial importance of recognizing one's self-worth. In *Mishnas Rav Aharon* (Volume One, p. 151), he explains that the essence of an individual's identity is based on his ability to recognize his importance. We learn this, Rav Aharon explains, from the following Talmudic passage: *Our Rabbis taught: He who eats in the marketplace is like a dog; and some say that he is unfit to testify* (*Kiddushin* 40b). Expanding on this Talmudic passage, the Rambam says that we can't accept the testimony of an individual who doesn't respect himself. Rav Aharon asks, "Why nullify the testimony of somebody who eats publicly? What does self-respect have to do with honesty?" He explains that the greatest deterrent to falsehood lies in asking oneself, *How can I do such a thing?* Without respect for oneself, one is not able to have proper respect for others. Such an individual can't be trusted to testify truthfully.

An episode that illustrates this point was told about a father who was concerned about the level of religious observance that his son would adhere to while attending graduate school away from his family and the intense Jewish environment in which he had been raised. He decided to bring his son to a rabbi for whom he had high regard to get a blessing before he left for the university. After giving the blessing the rabbi said that he would also like to give him advice on how to resist the temptations of living in a totally secular environment. Expecting advice that the university student should establish a relationship with a local rabbi who would be his teacher and mentor, the father and son were surprised when the rabbi suggested that he seek out a younger person to whom he would teach Torah. The rabbi explained that being a role model for somebody else would serve as an even greater motivator in keeping him loyal to Torah. If tempted to associate with the wrong friends and participate in unseemly activities, the graduate student would be restrained because he would be fearful that his student might see him and thereby lose respect for his teacher.

The Talmud in *Sanhedrin* (37a), marveling on the uniqueness of each individual, comments: *If a man mints many coins from one mold, they all resemble one another, but the supreme King of kings, the Holy One, Blessed is He, minted every man in the stamp of the first man, and yet not one of them resembles his fellowman. Therefore every single person is obliged to say, "The world was created for my sake."*

The obvious question regarding this statement is how one reconciles this with the necessity to be humble as typified by Abraham who said, *"I am but dust and ashes"* (*Genesis* 18:27).

In a well-known statement regarding reconciling the seeming contradiction between these two apparently competing imperatives, Rav Simcha Bunim from Peshichsa suggested that everybody needs to have two pockets that should be dipped into as needed: One pocket should contain the phrase, "The world was created for my sake," and the other should have the words, "I am but dust and ashes." The ideal balance in achieving an appropriate self-image is attained when individuals are able to reach into the appropriate pocket depending on the demands of the situation (*Simchas Yisrael, Mamorei Simcha,* Section 12).

Rabbi Shraga Feivel Mendlowitz, commenting on this insight of Rav Simcha Bunim, noted that people often reach into the wrong pocket at the wrong time. For example, when a person feels that he has been slighted by being given an honor in *shul* that he feels is beneath him, he reaches into the "The world was created for my sake" pocket and is inappropriately hurt and angry. When approached to do something for the community, however, he goes into the "I am but dust and ashes" pocket, claiming a false and misplaced sentiment that he isn't up to the job.

In an age of indulgence and entitlement it is important for parents to note the context in which the Talmud discusses the concept of "The world was created for my sake." The *mishnah* in *Sanhedrin* (37a) discusses this view of man in the context of a witness's responsibility to testify reliably and honestly. In an attempt to instill a sense of awe about a witness's responsibility in a capital case, the *mishnah* highlights the unique sanctity of each individual. The intention of teaching the concept of "The world was created for my sake" is, therefore, not to impart a sense of entitlement, but rather, to teach one's responsibility to others.[2]

◄ Parental Role:

Parents play a central role in the development of a child's self-esteem. They play a pivotal part in the following factors that have been found to influence a child's self-concept:[3]

1. A respectful, accepting attitude that children receive from others, particularly parents, is a key building block of a healthy sense of self. Repeatedly, studies have found that parents who provide a home that provides warmth, clear expectations, consistency and appropriate modeling are likely to raise children who experience high levels of self-esteem.[4]

2. The child's history of success and the resulting status that this earns the youngster at school and at home is another key force shaping a child's view of himself. A child's self-esteem is largely the result of the mirrors held back to him by family members, teachers and peers. A high level of self-esteem is likely when the reflected appraisals of others are positive.

3. How a child defines success or failure, as well as his general attitude toward negative feedback, is another important influence. This dynamic is shaped by both temperament and how the child is parented.

In addition to the forces that shape self-esteem, it is helpful to keep in mind that a child's self-concept is not a monolithic

---

[2] This *Dvar Torah* was told by Rabbi Hillel Davis.

[3] Coopersmith, S. (1967), *The Antecedents of Self-esteem,* San Francisco, CA: Freeman.

[4] Mruk, C. (1995), "Self-esteem: Research, Theory and Practice," New York: Springer.

concept. Psychologists describe the following dimensions that comprise self-esteem:

1. **Academic competence:** How "smart" a child feels himself to be relative to his peers. Since intelligence is made up of multiple domains, it is possible to feel that one shines in one area of intelligence and is relatively weak in another. For example, a child who is a brilliant writer may feel "dumb" if he has difficulty with math. This domain of self-concept is particularly important for Jewish children, who typically live in an environment that emphasizes academic skills above most other assets.

2. **Physical Appearance:** This is a particularly important source of self-esteem for girls. In a *shidduch* climate that often places inordinate emphasis on a girl's weight and general appearance, physical self-concept can be a major contributor to a girl's overall sense of worth. Research has shown that having a poor physical self-concept can be an important risk factor for eating disorders.

3. **Behavioral:** How a child views his behavior relative to peers is another component of self-concept. If a child views himself as "bad" he may be more likely to engage in rebellious behavior and is at increased risk for gravitating toward negative peer influences.

4. **Athletic:** In the Orthodox world, athletic ability is often not as major a force in shaping self-concept as in the general population. However, parents of young boys know that a child who is a poor athlete often feels badly about himself, particularly during his elementary school years.

5. **Social:** Feeling popular, particularly during adolescence — when fitting in with one's peer group is a major psychological need — is another major dimension of self-esteem.

Of course the sum can be greater than each of its parts. A child's global self-worth may be excellent, even if he suffers from a poor self-image in some of the above dimensions. The combination of a child's temperament, how his parents make him feel about himself and how much relative importance he assigns to a particular component of self-esteem will determine each child's overall self-image.

This approach to understanding self-esteem has several practical implications. Research has found that helping youngsters discount the importance of domains in which they are not competent or facilitating an improvement in their competence in areas where they are weak[5] are among the more effective ways of improving children's self-images. For example, in the case of children who are not particularly skilled athletes, self-esteem can improve by helping them see how, in the long run, this says nothing about their value as a person — while other areas of competence, such as academic skill or good character traits, are far more valuable assets. Another effective approach would be to give such an individual coaching that would improve his athletic skills. Of course, an approach using both of these strategies would have the best chance of improving the child's self-esteem.

ᐊᕈ Development of Self-concept:

Children's self-concepts become increasingly stable as they grow older. Until the typical child starts school he tends to view himself in an unrealistically positive and optimistic light. His true abilities have not been tested by day-to-day comparison to peers. Consequently, preschoolers will often describe themselves as being the "smartest" or "strongest," regardless of their true behavior and skills. Research finds that as children move through the early elementary school years their sense of competence sees a decline relative to the preschool years. Their sense of self becomes increasingly more objective and grounded as they forge a sense of relative confidence by comparing their abilities to those of their classmates.[6] In the laboratory of real life, young children come to gradually discover that they have strengths in some areas and weaknesses in others.

---

[5] Harter, S. (1999), *The Construction of the Self: A Developmental Perspective*, New York: Guilford Press.

[6] Cole, D., Maxwell, S. and Martin, J. (2001), "The Development of multiple domains of child and adolescent self-concept: a cohort sequential longitudinal design," *Child Development*, 72:1723-1746.

Self-concept gradually improves and stabilizes as children go through the later elementary school years. Parents should be aware, however, that there are various transition points where a child's sense of worth typically declines. This is especially true during the early adolescent years — a period often marked by insecurity and a lack of confidence. As the young teen undergoes the transition from elementary school to middle school and endures the stresses that often attend the onset of puberty, many domains of self-concept have been found to drop. A sense of confidence and competence typically reemerges during the latter years of high school. The above is only a very general map of how self-concept develops in a typical child. Any child who feels inferior to peers in academic ability, popularity, athletic skills, appearance or behavior will have low self-esteem in that area regardless of his or her stage of development. Despite competence, children who are raised in a home that is dominated by criticism, a punitive disciplinary style, or a failure to find a balance between love and limits will also be at risk for suffering the ill effects of a poor self-concept.

◄֎ Subtle Contributions to Self-Esteem

One of the most powerful contributors to self-esteem is a child's perception of what he is capable of doing. This is shaped both by the expectations of others, as well as the expectations he has of himself. In *Chovas HaTalmidim*, the Piacesner Rebbe asked his students to try to picture where they wanted to be in six months. He recognized that a child's dreams and aspirations are powerful forces that shape his ability to actualize his potential.

In one of the classic experiments in the field of psychology,[7] a group of researchers randomly chose one out of five elementary schoolchildren in 18 classrooms. Their teachers were told that these students were unusually bright and were expected to make

---

[7] Rosenthal, R. and Jackson, L. (1966), *Pygmalion in the Classroom: Expectation and Pupils' Intellectual Development.* New York: Holt, Rinehart & Winston.

remarkable progress during the coming academic year. Even though these children had no greater inherent potential than the other 80 percent of their classmates, they made unusual progress during the year that their teachers viewed them as gifted. Relative to their peers, significant increases in verbal skill, reasoning ability and overall intellectual ability were documented on intelligence and achievement tests that they were given at the end of the year.

The authors of this study speculate that expectations of children are transmitted in the most subtle of ways. Facial expressions, posture and tone of voice are all unconscious, yet powerful ways that communicate expectations. This is certainly the case with children. Parents often shape a child's view of what he can and can't do via the subtle expression of a raised eyebrow or an understated scowl. Setting appropriately high standards for one's children while, at the same time, not overwhelming them with inappropriately high expectations is an important ingredient in raising children with high levels of self-esteem.

◄ξ Cautions Regarding Self-esteem

In recent years there has been increasing concern that, in an age of plenty and indulgence, parents are raising children in such a child-centered manner that the pendulum has swung too far in the direction of overly heightened concern for a child's self-esteem. Critics have noted that in the name of self-esteem, children haven't been sufficiently exposed to the value of honest feedback or to recognize that the rewards and praise should be pegged to effort rather than to entitlement. Some evidence supporting the existence of this trend comes from surveys of how the members of the general population view their abilities relative to peers. Among the findings of these surveys are the following:

- Almost nobody in the United States rates him- or herself as having below-average leadership ability.
- Approximately 90 percent of Americans view themselves as above-average drivers.

- North American children who receive low scores on mathematics achievement tests rate their mathematical ability higher than Asian children who receive higher scores on the same tests.[8]

Harboring an overly inflated self-esteem is not without serious potential consequences. There is compelling evidence that an overinflated self-concept can lead to behavioral difficulties. Researchers have found that bullies and violent individuals often have an unrealistically positive view of themselves. When that highly favorable view is disputed or otherwise threatened by an individual or circumstance, they often lash out at anybody who is perceived as posing a threat to their sense of superiority.[9] Contrary to popular belief, it is the victims, not the perpetrators of violence, who are likely to suffer from poor self-concepts.

Recommendations:

■ Research on enhancing self-esteem in children has focused on two basic strategies. The first is improving skills in areas of weakness: Even the weakest student or the most uncoordinated athlete can be offered tutoring or coaching to help them make relative progress in areas of weakness. The second strategy is necessary when children have neither the ability nor motivation to improve in areas that impacts on their self-esteem. In such cases, parents can help their children learn to discount the importance of areas in which they feel inadequate while highlighting the importance of areas in which they are skilled. Susan Harter, a psychologist who is a leading authority on self-esteem in children, advocates helping the child "spend more 'psychological time' in those life niches where favorable self-appraisals

---

[8] Final Report of the California Task Force to Promote Self-Esteem and Personal and Social Responsibility, Bureau of Publications, California State Department of Education, Sacramento, CA (1990).

[9] Baumeinster, R., Smart, L. & Boden, J. (1996), "Relation of threatened egotism to violence and agression: the dark side of high self-esteem," *Psychological Review*, 103:5-33.

are more common, while helping the child avoid arenas in which he feels inadequate."[10]

■ Encouraging relatively accurate self-evaluations are generally in a child's best interest. Studies have shown that children who either significantly underestimate or significantly overestimate their abilities tend to avoid challenging tasks, while consistently choosing easier goals for themselves. The ideal is for children to set goals that are slightly above their level of comfort. This, the research indicates, tends to yield the best results and the highest levels of self-esteem.

Girls, in particular, are at risk for significantly underestimating their abilities.[11] An illusion of incompetence is often seen in girls, who then consistently fail to challenge themselves with tasks in which they clearly have the ability to excel. Parents should be particularly tuned in to this phenomenon in their daughters, who may be inappropriately dipping into the pocket of "I am but dust and ashes," when they should be challenging themselves by taking on the responsibility of "The world was created for my sake."

In general, in dealing with children who underrate their competence, parents should be aware that it is often an uphill battle to convince a child that he is more capable than he believes. Children often go to considerable lengths to maintain a negative view of themselves. Their automatic reaction will be to reject any feedback that they are, in fact, more capable than they believe. It takes effort, time and feedback to help a child become comfortable with a view of himself that doesn't fit his preconceived notions.

■ Until a child enters elementary school, parental emphasis should be on taking delight in and nurturing the child in a manner that conveys that he is wonderful and special, no matter what. While

---

[10] Harter, S. (1999), *The Construction of the Self: A Developmental Perspective*, p. 317, New York: Guilford Press.

[11] Phillips, D. and Zimmerman, M. (1990), "The Developmental Course of Perceived Competence and Incompetence Among Competent Children," in R. Sternberg and J. Kolligant (Eds.), *Competence Considered* (pp. 41-66), New Haven: Yale University Press.

parents may reprove or chastise a child for misbehaving, their disapproval should always refer to the behavior, never to the child himself. Love and approval at that age must be unconditional. The goal is to engender positive self-esteem that is not contingent on the approval of others.

- Keep in mind that young children (under age 6) even when exposed to repeated failure tend to consistently overrate their abilities. This is a normal part of child development stemming from a combination of the cognitive immaturity and a lack of experience in comparing themselves to others. Parents should accept such behavior as part of a preschooler's maturation process. There is no need for concern or intervention.

- Periods of major transition are often accompanied by significant drops in a child's self-esteem. Research has documented such periods of vulnerability when a child begins middle school and at the beginning of high school. The bright side of this process is that the new opportunities offered by these settings also present new prospects for growth in feelings of competence. Parents can facilitate this process by offering additional emotional support and encouraging appropriate assumptions of new challenges during these periods of transition.

- Parental approval or disapproval of the essence of a child's personality is probably the most important contributor to a sense of one's self as being worthy and competent. In an effort to maximize feelings of independence, adolescents may resist fully utilizing their parents as sources of support. The parents' role is to find a zone of comfort that enables their adolescent to lean on them for support and confidence without feeling smothered or infantilized. Please remember that many adolescents acknowledge needing parental support and approval, even when their overt behavior may suggest that they prefer to be left alone by their parents.

- When an adolescent is unable to fully utilize parental support to feel better about themselves, parents should consider facilitating recruitment of other adults. Research consistently shows that most adolescents are able to benefit tremendously from the support of grandparents, aunts, uncles, teachers and rebbis, or parents of their friends. Parents should view such sources of support as important allies in the process of building their child's self-esteem, rather than as competitors for their child's affection.

■ Acceptance by peers is a major contributor to the self-esteem of children and adolescents. In some cases, an insecure or pessimistic child may simply be underestimating the level of support he receives from peers. Encouragement from parents to view one's social support system more realistically is the obvious strategy in dealing with a child who views himself as unpopular when, in fact, he has many friends.

When a child accurately views himself as unpopular, the role of parents depends on the source of these difficulties. In cases where the rejection seems to be based on a deficit in the child's social skills, parents should consult mental health professionals to determine the best way of teaching the child how to improve his or her social skills. The range of services offered by such professionals includes social-skills training groups; individual, behaviorally oriented psychotherapy; and/or consultation with the school to best help diagnose and intervene to improve a child's social situation.

At times, the situation is not based on a deficit in social skills, but on a child having to deal with a group of peers who have formed exclusive cliques or are cruel or rejecting. In such cases the child may need help in finding a new group of friends while at the same time strategies can be developed to help him or her avoid the group of nonsupportive peers. In extreme situations, once it is determined that the social problem lies more in the peer group than in the child, it might be necessary to either switch classes or — if absolutely necessary — find him or her a new school. On a number of occasions I (DP) have found that when a child who is rejected socially in one school is given a fresh start with a new group of peers in a different school or neighborhood, he or she blossoms socially. This, of course, can do wonders for such a child's self-esteem. It is crucial, of course, before taking such a drastic step, that parents make sure that the social difficulty does not stem from a child-based deficit in social skills. Obviously, in such a situation, enrolling in a new school will only result in another negative experience for the child, which will inevitably lead to an even greater sense of failure and rejection.

■ The ultimate goal for parents is to insure that their children's self-concept is based on an internalized sense of themselves as worthy and competent rather than on a sense of worthiness that is contingent on the approval of others. When children's self-esteem is based solely on the approval of others, they are likely to experience wide fluctuations in the way they view themselves, as they are at the whim of the opinion of friends and acquaintances.

Children are at risk of developing a false sense of self-esteem when they are raised by a family that relies on "impression management" — a sense that one has to continually live up to the externally imposed standards of others.[12] An extreme example of this was described to me by a colleague who had a client who couldn't afford air-conditioning in his car but who forced his family to drive with the windows closed during the summer months lest people view them as not being able to afford air-conditioning. Such contingent self-esteem is by its very nature fragile and transitory. In contrast, parents should try to teach their children to establish personal ideals toward which they strive, and to evaluate present performance in relation to their own past performance. When children are helped to focus on an internal sense of standards, i.e., to match or exceed their "personal best," rather than to constantly compare themselves to others, they are well on their way to establishing a healthy sense of self-esteem.

A related goal is to teach children that **effort** is rewarded — not just success. By rewarding effort rather than outcome parents help a child learn to have a healthy sense of self that is not contingent on the vagaries of outside approval.

■ Expectations of children from whom one does not anticipate much can be communicated in a number of subtle ways, most

---

[12] Deci, E. and Ryan, R. (1995), "Human Autonomy: The Basis for True Self-Esteem," in M. Kernis (Ed.), *Efficacy, Agency and Self-Esteem* (pp. 31-46), New York: Plenum.

of which a parent may not consciously recognize. Examples of how parents might unwittingly deliver such messages include:

a. Waiting less time for a child to give an answer than one would to a sibling for whom one has higher expectations.

b. Criticizing low-expectation children for failure more often and more severely than high-expectation children, and praising them less frequently for success.

c. Paying less attention to low-expectation children during family discussions. This can take the form of asking more stimulating, higher-level questions to a sibling from whom one expects more. It can also present by responding to the low-expectation children with briefer and less informative answers to their questions.

d. Beware of subtle nonverbal cues. Parents communicate a lack of confidence when studying with children from whom they expect less, if they respond to their answers with a diminished level of smiling, positive head nodding, forward leaning and eye contact.

Afterword

In writing this book we were guided by years of input from the numerous parents who have turned to us for counsel. The topics covered reflect the recurring concerns that we have encountered. We recognize that there are numerous important issues that were not discussed in this volume. For example, the challenges of single parents, the issue of abuse and molestation and of substance abuse were not systematically addressed. Hopefully in the future these critical parenting challenges will be given the attention they deserve.

A story is told of a man who comes into a store to buy a compass. The clerk asks him: "What kind of compass do you want? Are you interested in drawing a circle or in finding your way?" What we have attempted to do is give our readers the type of compass that will help them find their way in navigating the often turbulent and confusing seas of parenting. This is especially essential in a society where so many parents find themselves going around in circles rather than discovering a direct, positive parenting path. We hope we have been successful in providing you with a proper compass.